DESIGNING AND CREATING JAPANESE GARDENS

PENNY UNDERWOOD

THE CROWOOD PRESS

First published in 2005 by
The Crowood Press Ltd
Ramsbury, Marlborough
Wiltshire SN8 2HR

www.crowood.com

British Library Cataloguing-in-Publication Data
A catalogue record for this book is available from the British Library.

ISBN 1 86126 783 5

Typeset and designed by D & N Publishing
Hungerford, Berkshire.

Printed and bound in Singapore by Craft Print International.

Contents

'Cedar Moss Garden'.
Yoshiki-en, Nara.

Preface

A highlight of my personal journey through a career in horticulture has been the writing of *Designing and Creating Japanese Gardens*. Opportunities have arisen along the way, as have some disappointments.

Always aware that there was something special about Japanese gardens, it seemed a distant dream that I would ever experience them first-hand. As a believer that the human psyche and welfare are strongly influenced by their environment, I did not realize that the peace and tranquillity engendered by Japanese gardens was of the essence. When a friend suggested a visit to the Far East, Hong Kong, Thailand and perhaps Bali, my response was 'Can we try to go to Japan to see the gardens?' This we did.

Despite the long flight, on our arrival in Kyoto the feeling of urgency to visit as many gardens as possible in a few days saw us walking through the city to the Imperial Household Office to arrange visits to the four Imperial Gardens in and around the city. Entering the first garden had a profound emotional and intellectual effect on me, which lasted for several months, and, to a lesser extent, has endured to this day.

That first visit was timed to coincide with the famous autumnal colours, the crystal-clear blue skies forming the perfect backdrop to the reds, oranges and yellows. After the visit, a burning desire to return to Japan and experience more gardens was fulfilled eighteen months later with a spring visit to pursue the pink flush of 'cherry blossoms' from Morioka and Kakunodate in the north of Honshu, to Kyoto further south, passing through Tokyo, Nikko and Kanazawa.

During this second visit a pre-arranged day was spent in the company of Yasutaro-Tanaka, a renowned Kyoto designer, who showed us several of the gardens created by his landscape gardening company. Tanaka-san had also designed and constructed well-known gardens in the United Kingdom, including a Zen garden at St Mungo's Museum in Glasgow, and the Kyoto Garden in Holland Park, London. I asked him whether it had been possible to obtain plants trained and pruned in the unique Japanese styles for these projects. 'No', was the reply. This precipitated a passionate quest to spend more time in Japan learning the specialist techniques.

The amount of time I felt justified in allocating to this project was six to eight weeks. Leaving my design and consultancy business for this length of time would mean a reduction in income, so the long quest for financial help began. Numerous applications for grant funding and several disappointments later, I received a generous offer from the Daiwa Anglo-Japanese Foundation in London, followed by an even more generous bursary from the Royal Horticultural Society, who were interested in the subject. My thanks to both these bodies for providing me with most of the funding to consider embarking on the study tour.

My friend Yukiko Ishida, whom I met while taking Japanese language classes in England, had returned to Japan and was aware of my dream. Unknown to me, she had spoken to Tanaka-san and he offered to help. What an offer! Free accommodation, some meals, and the opportunity to study and work with his teams of designers and skilled gardeners whenever appropriate. This also meant that I was left time to explore on my own and travel to other parts of Japan. My eternal thanks to Ishida-san and to Tanaka-san, his family and experienced staff who generously shared their knowledge with me – a *gaijin* and female!

In late October 1997, with some trepidation, I set off for a wonderful six weeks of information gathering and garden visiting, forming firm friendships with many whom I met, returning with treasured memories, copious notes and some 1,600 photographs. Stowed in my luggage were several books, a bamboo pruning saw, pruning shears and other sundry gardening items. My writing about the gardens of Japan was launched while I was attending a meeting of the Institute of Horticulture shortly before the second trip to Japan. The editor of the Institute's journal, *The Horticultulist*, asked me to write a piece on my return. The following year I was commissioned by the Royal Horticultural Society to write an article for *The Garden*. Other requests for series of articles came from the editor of *The Art of Bonsai – Incorporating Japanese Gardens* and *Koi Carp Magazine*. My thanks to Barbara Segall for suggesting that I write that first article, and to all the other editors with whom I have worked.

My thanks also to the Foundation to Preserve the Nishida Family Garden for allowing me to reproduce material on the Gyokusen-en garden in Kanazawa, and to Jason Hayter for his beautiful illustrations.

Finally, my thanks to friends and associates who have encouraged me throughout the writing process, and have been patient when there has been no time or energy to share with them.

On leaving Japan at the end of the study tour, the parting words of Yano-san, a Japanese designer who had generously shared a wealth of knowledge with me were, 'please show Western people what a Japanese garden is really like.' I hope that this has been achieved and that readers will be inspired to discover more for themselves.

1

Introduction to History, Philosophy and Spirituality

To experience the gardens of Japan can profoundly affect the psyche of those who have the opportunity of crossing the threshold into these wondrous places. Their deep spirituality has evolved over many centuries and can be traced through the history of Japan and its people; but in the West some glaring misconceptions about Japanese gardens have been perpetuated which fail to do justice to their philosophical roots and evolving design styles.

Japanese gardens, of whatever era or style, express the beliefs of their creators, illustrating their understanding of the natural world in design concepts, as well as encompassing the spiritual beliefs of the time, using and manipulating the materials at their disposal and thereby interpreting the natural world in an unnatural setting, the balance of natural and manmade elements forming their aesthetic basis; *teien*, a Japanese word for garden, may be broadly interpreted as the opposites of wildness and control.

Early Influences

The archipelago we know as Japan (*Nihon*, the land of the rising sun) was formed by the movement of the tectonic plates which rim the Pacific Ocean. The spine of Japan was formed from molten magma forced through underwater fissures and creating numerous volcanoes and associated hot water springs. Three-quarters of Japan's landmass is mountainous, with steep valleys and narrow coastal plains and the geology of the resultant island chain, and the plants which colonized it, were and are important factors in shaping Japanese life in general and garden design in particular. The early settlers of the islands were probably migrants from China and Korea. The first sightings of this volcanic landscape would have been of rugged islands rising from the sea, sometimes shrouded in mists or clouds which added to their mystique. The warming after the last Ice Age gradually changed the character of this island chain from a largely inhospitable environment to one which became home to a spectrum of plants similar to that which we know today. Human habitation became possible and the creation of Japanese gardens began.

The pioneer Chinese settlers took with them an established culture of creating gardens which was incorporated into Japanese garden design, reinterpreted over the ensuing centuries, yet the resulting Japanese garden styles are distinctive, and so too is the architectural detail of the buildings with which many gardens are associated.

OPPOSITE PAGE:
'Cloud pruned' Cupressus. Momoyama Castle, Kyoto.

Spirituality and Philosophy

Spirituality in Japanese garden design can be traced back to prehistoric times. It has been popularly thought that the native Japanese religion of Shinto was based on animism which believed that rocks and plants had human qualities and that special places in the landscape, such as waterfalls, islands, old trees or protruding boulders, were inhabited by the gods – *kami*. An opposing view is that the natural world is an intrinsic part of a godly whole which is manifested in a variety of spiritual, psychic and physical states, and that particularly powerful places and objects inspire communication with the all-embracing, single god. Whichever is the true basis of the belief system, the special sites were, and still are, treated with reverence and usually festooned with straw or paper garlands.

Whether myth or legend, there was a belief that the native gods of Japan either descended from above or came from over the sea. Sacred stones – *iwa-kura* – were designated for the former and sacred ponds – *kami-ike* – for the latter.

Sacred sequoia with rice-straw garland. Kokedera Temple, Kyoto.

Taoist Myths and Legends

Taoist legends imported by the early settlers told of islands populated by those who attained immortality and lived together in perfect harmony, and who, it was claimed, were carried on the backs of cranes. The islands, in turn, were carried on the backs of giant sea turtles. It is said that Japan was enchanted by this myth and that the islands of Chinese legend were condensed and symbolized in Japanese garden design as a mountain called *Horai* and, sometimes as crane (*tsuru-jima*) or turtle (*kame-jima*) islands. Crane islands are usually mounds, with rocks or pine trees depicting a bird in flight. Turtle islands, which nestle in water or sand, are small mounds with a rock resembling the head, four less prominent rocks as the feet, and sometimes another for a tail. The longevity of cranes and turtles thereby became translated into a garden setting.

Symbolic Places

Revered Rocks

There may be other explanations for crane and turtle islands. Rock shapes are endowed with significance. The 'Never Aging Rock' is considered to be similar to a newly formed mountain which has not been exposed to centuries of weathering; its steep, jagged profile being reminiscent of a crane in flight. Whereas 'The Rock of Ten Thousand Aeons' has succumbed

Rocks arranged in 'turtle' formation. National Park, Nikko.

Weathered stones, representing islands of the ancient Orient. Southern Garden of hojo. *Tofuku-ji Temple, Kyoto.*

BELOW: *Unweathered stones, representing islands of the more recent Occident. Southern Garden of* hojo. *Tofuku-ji Temple, Kyoto.*

to the effects of wind and weather, eventually becoming rounded like the shell of a turtle.

This contrast in rock shapes also perpetuates the belief that Eastern habitats and civilizations were formed before those in the West. This is a belief strongly symbolized in a twentieth-century garden within the Tofuku-ji Temple complex in Kyoto, where a grouping of softly round stones representing the Orient, is set in a symbolic ocean and reaches out westwards to more sharply defined landforms representing the less ancient Occident.

As Taoism and Shintoism gave way to Buddhism in Japan, the use of rocks in garden design continued, but now the symbolism was directed towards Buddhist beliefs, becoming an important foundation of social and aesthetic life.

One of the images was of the legendary mountain *Shumisen*. It was believed that *Shumisen* was surrounded by eight rings of lower mountains with eight seas between them. The outermost ring was the habitat of man, and depictions of this fantasy involved a central prominent stone surrounded by smaller ones.

Horai and *Shumisen* may well have been mountains of fantasy. One of the sights most evocative of Japan is that of Mount Fuji, majestically rising above the main island of Honshu. Fuji-san holds a special place in the hearts of the Japanese whose very survival depends on the quiescence of the volcano within. Mount Fuji has also gained recognition through the centuries in varying design styles, up to and including the twentieth century.

ABOVE: Rock groupings and grassy representation of
Mt Fuji, Donnington Park, near Newbury, England.

BELOW: Phoenix Hall, with bridge
connection to the 'shore'. Byodo-in, Uji.

Rock and azalea grouping of Amida Nyorai and twenty-five Bodhisattvas, with clouds for receiving the souls of the dying. Chion-in Temple, Kyoto.

Sanzon-seki-gumi, *stone arrangement. Private garden, Inari area of Kyoto.*

A powerful Buddhist image reproduced in garden design was the 'Pure Land' or paradise of Amida Buddha. It is believed that Amida Buddha lives in and presides over the Pure Land, to which the spirits of enlightened individuals rise after death and are thus freed from the cycle of death and rebirth in the struggle to gain nirvana. The garden of Byodo-in in Uji, south of Kyoto, illustrates the Pure Land image with the central hall standing on an island in the 'sea', with bridge connections to the 'shore', implying the potential for all mortals to attain the Pure Land.

In the East garden of *Kōhōjo* of Chion-in Temple in Kyoto, the 'Pure Land' is romanticized in a setting of twenty-five green rocks symbolizing the twenty-five Bodhisattvas who attend Amida Nyorai, mingled with azalea bushes indicating the long-tailed, fast-flying clouds on which the Bodhisattvas ride when receiving the souls of the dying.

Not least among the rock groupings associated with Buddhist beliefs are *sanzon-seki*, consisting of three carefully chosen rocks, set in a triangular arrangement sometimes representing man, heaven and earth. More often such arrangements symbolize a Buddhist trilogy (*sanzon-seki-gumi*) with the largest depicting Shaka or Amida Nyorai Buddha, with the two smaller, flanking stones representing their attendants.

Hallowed Water

Water is also endowed with divine properties, without it all would perish. Historically, Japanese settlers were particularly aware of this dependence – rivers, lakes and the sea provided a multitude of fish. Similarly rivers, punctuated with

Rocky islands in the 'sea'. Osawa Ike, the largest pond to have survived since the ninth century. North-west of Kyoto.

BELOW: *Written character for 'heart' (top) and* Kokoro *pond at Saiho-Ji Temple, Kyoto (bottom).*

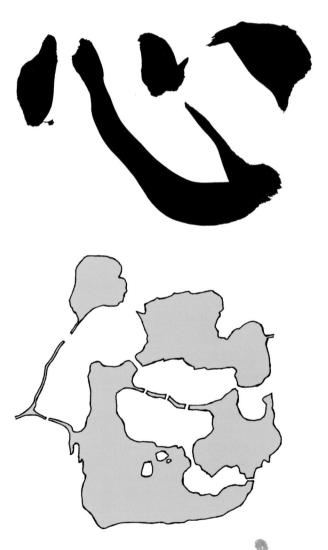

waterfalls and rocky outcrops, supplied the water for growing food crops and in particular rice, the staple Japanese food. Hot water for bathing was, and still is, abundantly supplied by the network of hot springs typical of volcanically active terrain. It is not surprising that a deeply spiritual culture would perceive water as a habitat and shrine for the gods. The natural springs which flowed into rivers or ponds were believed to be the source of life in which the gods dwelt. *Kami-ike* (divine ponds) therefore became shrines to the gods that inhabited the well spring, in addition to those which came from the sea. The use of water in Japanese garden design is traceable back to prehistoric times and sacred places. *Kami-ike* and *iwa-kura* were originally built as Shinto shrines; sacred places for prayers and rituals. Their aesthetic values were later incorporated into garden designs.

One of the earliest writings on Japanese garden design and construction, the *Sakuteiki*, written in the twelfth century, instructs that 'the pond should be dug in the shape of a turtle or crane ... the shape of the pond itself affects the good or evil omen'. 'The pond may also be in the form of some auspicious word written in the cursive style.' In Chinese and Japanese script ideograms often draw a picture of the objects they describe, some of which have been translated into pond shapes such as water, *mizu*, and heart, *kokoro*. It was recommended that the flow of water into a pond should be from the north-east, running to the south-west, allowing the power of the eastern Blue Dragon to wash out evils that could be blocking the way of the western White Tiger.

Crossings over ponds and streams also became significant as guards against unwelcome spirits. As it was believed that evil spirits could cross water only in straight lines, several styles of zigzag bridge were developed. Stepping stones

Early screen painting of rocky 'landscape'.
Daisen-in Temple, Daitoku-ji, Kyoto.

Kare-sansui, *adjacent to the* hojo.
Ryogen-in Temple, Daitoku-ji, Kyoto.

(*sawatari-ishi*), of either irregular or uniform shape, were placed randomly at footfall spacing, wending across the water.

Kare-Sansui

Many of the early gardens were built in cool foothills with readily available supplies of water. With the growth of settlements in valleys, as in Kyoto, the inclusion of water in gardens remained equally important but less practicable and thus the concept of dry gardens developed throughout the middle ages. By the sixteenth century the 'withered mountain water' – *kare-sansui* – had emerged as a new garden prototype, especially for those gardens built within the confines of urban Zen temples. Zen Buddhism advocates meditation as a journey to enlightenment, seeing beyond the superficial aspects of life in order to perceive a greater truth and peace. Replacing water with gravel ensured that Buddhist beliefs could be skilfully represented in dry gardens, particularly in confined areas around temple buildings.

Inspiration was drawn from the monochromatic drawings of Taoist China, where ideas of man's place in nature ran close to Zen ideas about existence. Zen designers looked for ways to represent the vastness of nature and life as the Chinese artists had done. Powerful images of mountains, glens, waterfalls and oceans were implied in very limited spaces, the environs of such gardens emptying the mind of other influences and inducing an intense focus on the symbolism portrayed.

Within the *kare-sansui* gardens was developed a technique familiar in the West, that of raking the gravel 'seas' into stylized shapes, thus suggesting fast flowing currents or eddies around islands. When visitors are welcomed to a temple and other complexes to experience these dry gardens, the raked gravels or sands are immaculate and seemingly inviolable. All is illusion. The structured patterns are disturbed by heavy rainfall and do not escape the debris of surrounding plant life, especially in autumn at leaf fall. Early each morning the monks or other custodians venture into these venerated places, removing all debris and raking the surfaces again. By these acts the participants express their contemplative life.

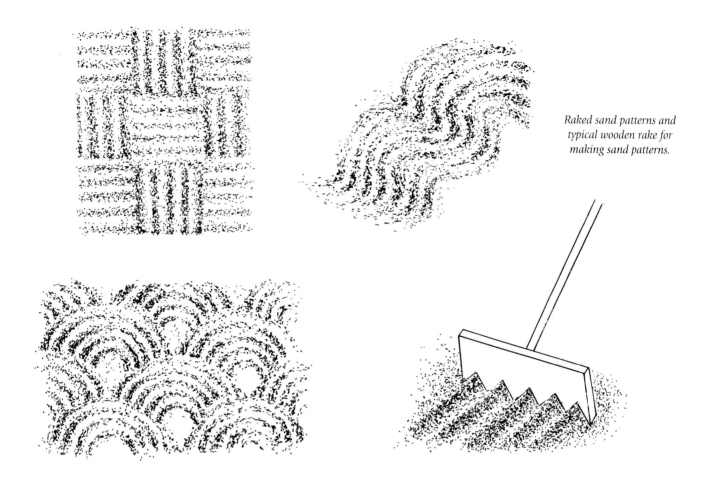

Raked sand patterns and typical wooden rake for making sand patterns.

Cleansing Water

In addition to its symbolic significance, whether real or perceived, water has more a fundamental and simpler use in Japanese garden design. As well as being recognized as a vital life-giving element, water is seen to possess powers to cleanse mind, body and soul. Traditionally, at the entrance to a shrine or temple, there will be a source of fresh mountain water which feeds into a receptacle, usually made of carved granite.

Worshippers stop to make use of the cleansing water before entering the place of worship to pray or give thanks.

With the advent of tea ceremony gardens (*roji* – dewy path) in the sixteenth century, the significance of cleansing water has developed. To help to create the right mood of cleanliness the tea master sprinkles the garden with water before the guests arrive. Ideally, in the passage through the garden to the tea house there will be a well, indicating the availability of fresh water for tea-making. As visitors draw nearer to the tea house, they approach a *tsukubai*: a grouping of water spout, water basin with ladle and accompanying stone arrangement. Once again, the cleansing water will be taken. It is important that participants need to bend in order to partake of the water, thus all are made equal and can enter the tea house and share the tea ceremony on an equal footing.

Granite water basin at entrance to shrine. Nikko.

Covered well.
Private garden, Kyoto.

Granite water basin with bamboo water
spout and ladle. Daitoku-ji Temple, Kyoto.

Plants and Symbolism

The availability of fresh water facilitates the growth of plants vital to man's existence. Plants in Japanese garden design are endowed with symbolic and philosophical properties and are treated with due respect.

There is a great diversity of plants native to the country, many of which are familiar in the West. The three groups which first come to mind are pines, maples and bamboos, each with their particular roles within Japanese gardens.

'Pines'

In Japanese the word for pine – *matsu* – is pronounced in the same way as the verb to wait. In the Heian period (794–1185*) pines implied waiting for a lover or resolving a difficult situation. Pines also suggest longevity, probably

stemming from the ancient image of pine-clad and revered mountains. Their refined character, with straight, evergreen needles, also indicates a proud spirit with the courage to survive harsh winters and possessing a dignity which is admired by the Japanese. Their ability to survive on craggy mountainsides or windswept islands is translated into garden settings. Pines are trained from young saplings to resemble those heroes of the plant world and are planted at precarious angles reflecting their native habitats.

The evocation of the natural habitat threads through Japanese garden design and the practice survives of planting trees from deep mountains in the 'deep mountains' represented in the garden; trees from hills and fields in the 'hills and fields' and trees from freshwater areas and sea shores in their individual environments. In particular, the Japanese red pine – *Pinus densiflora*, and Japanese black pine – *Pinus thunbergii* – are planted to symbolize mountains and seashore.

By contrast, a shaping/pruning technique often employed on pines and other species is that which has become known as 'cloud pruning', where layered 'pads' of growth are

---

NOTE
* All dates are Christian era.

TOP: *'Windswept'* Pinus. *Private garden, Sagano area, Kyoto.*

ABOVE: *Trained* Pinus thunbergii. *Ritsurin Koen, Takamatsu.*

developed over many years forming a helix around the trunk, sometimes referred to as a 'stairway to heaven', suggesting that there is a heavenly place which souls can reach by ascending above the 'clouds'.

In man's quest for longevity, the evergreen pines held a particular significance for the ancient Chinese and Japanese who believed that drinking the sap of a 3,000-year-old pine would give a lifespan of 500 years to the partaker. Whether there is any evidence for this belief is a matter for conjecture. Pines are considered to be one of the 'Three Friends of Winter' which give hope for the future.

Seasonal Symbolic Plants

Unlike Western gardens, a patchwork of flowering plants and all-year-round colour do not feature in Japan. However, some flowering plants and colourful foliage are given pride of place and, in contrast to the 'permanence' of pines and other conifers, are used to signify the passing of the seasons.

Considered to be another of 'The Three Friends of Winter' is the earliest of these, the flowering plum – *Prunus mume* – *ume*, is said to promise rebirth and the renewal of vitality and hope and is often planted adjacent to garden or temple entrances where the sweetly perfumed flowers can be enjoyed by those who pass by.

As the year progresses, during April and May, Japan bursts into a flush of pink from south to north when the cherry blossoms open. The daintiness of the individual flowers, silhouetted against blue spring skies, have given flowering

ABOVE: Prunus mume *and bell tower. Entrance to temple, Nikko.*

Blossom viewing. Morioka.

Ancient Prunus mume *overhanging wooden perimeter fence of samurai house. Kakunodate.*

cherries – *sakura* – a special place in the hearts of the Japanese since the eighth century when their natural beauty began to be recognized by the nobility. Blossom-viewing parties – *o-hanami* – became more and more popular and today, are enjoyed by the entire nation.

The samurai believed that 'The soul of *sakura* is the soul of *bushido* [chivalry] and the heart of *bushido* is the heart of Japan'. The samurai expected to die voluntarily, like the cherry blossoms blown away on sudden spring breezes.

The native camellias are also widely used in Japanese gardens either as specimens or in groups, sometimes as hedges. Spring-flowering *Camellia japonica* has large flower heads which typically do not fall off petal by petal but as a whole, a characteristic seen by the samurai as a bad omen, resembling the falling of human heads in battle. The flowers of the fragrant, autumn-flowering *Camellia sasanqua* are, however, less threatening since they do fall petal by petal.

Where there is a pond or stream, there will almost inevitably be plantings of irises, most commonly of *Iris kaempferi*, syn. *I. ensata*, which flowers in May and June. The fresh, pointed spikes arising from clear waters, are thought to

Camellia japonica and Sasa veitchii. *Garden of samurai house, Kakunodate.*

Iris kaempferi *in stream. Jonangu-ji, Kyoto.*

ABOVE: *Lotus bud motif. Lacquered bridge, Momoyama Castle, Kyoto.*

Maple glen viewed from covered bridge. Tofuku-ji Temple, Kyoto.

symbolize man's triumphant passage into the light from the murky, muddy waters encountered through life's journey.

In the heat of August the more flamboyant lotus – *Nelumbo nucifera* – flowers in abundance in wet habitats. Endowed with similar characteristics to those of the iris, the flowers and leaves of the lotus are frequently depicted in artefacts and paintings within and around Buddhist temples and other important buildings. To sit on the Lotus Throne symbolizes rebirth in paradise after death, and is a goal of the Buddhist faith.

As summer fades into autumn, the hills and glens are ablaze with colourful foliage; the most spectacular being the maples which are the main ingredients of the Japanese autumn and often planted to resemble a natural woodland. For centuries maples have infiltrated the psyche and gardens of the Japanese. During the Edo period (1603–1867) the interest and enthusiasm heightened, with maple-viewing parties, a tradition which continues today.

ABOVE: Autumn colouring, Acer palmatum. *Kokedera, Kyoto.*

TOP RIGHT: Autumn foliage, Ginkgo biloba *'Princeton Sentry'. Arashiyama area, Kyoto.*

RIGHT: Fallen Ginkgo biloba *leaves on stepping stones. Hakusasonsō Garden, Kyoto.*

The Japanese refer to maples as '*kaede*' or, more commonly, '*momiji*'; the first from the words for 'frog hand' and refers to the similarity of lobed foliage to the webbed hand of a frog, and *momiji*, more whimsically, translates as 'little baby extends his tiny hands which are like the leaves of maple'. Another descriptive interpretation of *momiji* is 'leaves become crimson', an accurate, although understated truism.

At the same time that maples turn to red and orange, the ginkgos turn to gold, their leathery leaves trembling in the autumn breeze, before falling to create a golden carpet below. *Ginkgo biloba* is one of the oldest trees known to man and thereby signifies longevity. There are many old and respected ginkgo trees associated with Shinto shrines, identified with *shime-nawa* ropes or folded white papers.

As the year ends, the third 'Friend of Winter', bamboo, stands proudly against the winter weather. The characteristic strength of bamboo, as well as its ability to bend in the breeze without breaking, its leaves quivering in the wind but not falling, is known in Japan as 'bamboo mentality', and the sign of a true gentleman: to yield, to return, retaining the ability to go forward unbroken by adversity. Due to its prominence in Asia, bamboo has featured for centuries in Chinese ink drawings and scroll paintings. There were painters who specialized in representations of bamboo, many of whom lived in the thirteenth century. Poetic verses often accompanied the spiritual ink drawings which accurately captured the character of bamboo. The bamboo artists believed that 'in order to paint bamboo you must become bamboo'.

Although botanically not a bamboo, a plant of great significance regularly planted in Japanese gardens is *Nandina domestica* – often referred to as 'Heavenly bamboo'. It is believed to bring good fortune to all who pass by it and therefore may be positioned in the north-east corner of a garden to aid the clearing of the way for the western White Tiger. Alternatively, it may be placed beside doorways, the bright red berries 'lighting' the way home.

Other berry-bearing shrubs are reputed to bring money and other riches: *Chloranthus glaber*, named by the Japanese as *senryo*, *ryo* being an old, gold coin and *sen* meaning one thousand. Even more wealth is bestowed upon those who nurture the coral berry – *Ardisia crenata* – otherwise known as *manryo*: *man* indicating ten thousand of the lucky golden coins.

Myths and legends, philosophical and spiritual beliefs, weave their way through the design of Japanese gardens over the centuries, which, like bamboo, retain their intrinsic dignity while bending with the times.

'*Hedge*' *of* Phyllostachys nigra.
Jonangu-ji Temple, Kyoto.

Nandina domestica *in small shop-front garden, Kyoto.*

2

Changing Styles through the Centuries

The Earliest Gardens (pre-710)

Although there are several literary references to gardens in Japan from as early as the first century, there is little tangible evidence from those times surviving today. In common with most cultures, the early settlers would have been hunter-gatherers, possibly nomadic, moving with the seasons to forage and find shelter. As the transition towards a more settled agrarian society gradually evolved, changes in attitude and lifestyle included the development of the cultural and physical environment. The necessity to provide food and shelter from a static location placed demands on the available land, where crops were tended and livestock nurtured. Simple shelters were superseded by farmhouses designed to accommodate the necessary chores in inclement weather.

Front gardens – *niwa* – and the work areas within the farmhouses – *doma* – although functional in essence, also embraced ceremonial and spiritual rituals. For instance, at the New Year the *doma* would be decorated with rice cakes to honour the gods of fire and water.

With the arrival of Chinese and Korean images brought by early travellers and settlers, the design of gardens gradually became more sophisticated. During the seventh century the Japanese sent official envoys, students, scholars and translators to study the culture of China. Cultural exchanges continued until the late ninth century, when Japan severed diplomatic and cultural relations with China. However, the assimilation of the cultures over the preceding two centuries created lasting influences on the social structures of Japan, many of which have endured to the present, including the use of land and the design of gardens.

Nara Period (710–794)

The earliest garden design styles of which there are verifiable records were in the Nara period. During this period, land began to pass into the possession of shrines, temples and aristocratic families. Journeying between their widespread manors, the aristocrats became more aware of the natural scenery through which they passed, and interpretations of those experiences expanded the concept of replicating the natural environment in a garden 'scene'.

Gardens of this period included 'Gardens by the Winding Stream' – *kyokusei-tei*. A recently rediscovered and reconstructed garden in Nara City, the ancient capital of Japan, was once part of the Imperial Palace garden and is typical of the style. A stream winds from north to south, between pebble 'beaches' and windswept pines, reminiscent of rugged rivers tumbling through the hills.

OPPOSITE PAGE:
Stream passing through Ryuten-tei,
Tea House. Koraku-en, Okayama.

'Gardens by the Winding Stream'. Imperial Palace Garden, Nara.

BELOW: 'Festival by the Winding Stream'. Jonangu-ji Shrine, Kyoto.

Heian Period (794–1185)

Winding Stream Gardens

During the Heian period gardens developed further. The 'winding stream' garden was perpetuated on a somewhat grander scale, gently weaving its way through the garden, usually fed from a natural water source. A courtly festival was, and still is, held along the stream banks – *kyokusui-no-en* – 'Festival by the Winding Stream', in which wooden ducks, carrying cups of sake, float downstream, and local notaries endeavour to compose poems to exchange for the passing of cups of sake: no poem, no sake. Islands, or specially built platforms, would be the stages for musicians and dancers clad in traditional costumes.

Pond-Touring Gardens

During the Heian period other styles of garden provided places for entertainment, and most notably those associated with grand palaces, often located in the countryside or on the outskirts of developing settlements. Designers of the 'pond-touring gardens' – *chisen shūyū teien* – created large, open pathways around ponds, along which guests would stroll and admire different aspects of the garden as the

Boat house beside lake. Shugaku-in Imperial Villa garden, Kyoto.

Viewing bench beside lake. Shugaku-in Imperial Villa garden, Kyoto.

meandering paths revealed ever changing views. Such gardens were elegant and colourful, inspiring visitors to express a heightened love of nature through poetry and music.

Contemporary writings confirm that boating parties assembled to indulge their fascination with the passing seasons. Parties would be rowed across the ponds in brightly decorated boats which they had boarded from stone steps or wooden jetties, destined for a fishing pavilion, a bird-watching hide or simply to sit on a covered bench and admire the view.

In addition to being accessible by boat, the low-lying islands were linked to the gardens in such a way that the festive boats could circumnavigate the islands.

'Shinden'-Style Gardens

During the Heian period the city of Heian-kyo was laid out on a grid system similar to that of its near neighbour

Nara, both based on Chinese models. The city which we know today as Kyoto superseded Nara as the nation's capital in 749.

The valley in which Kyoto lies is bounded by mountains to the west, north and east, the Takano River runs from the north-eastern corner southwards through modern-day Kyoto and exits to the south-west, having merged with the Kamo and the Katsura River, thus conforming to the legend of the Blue Dragon clearing the way for the White Tiger. The north-east corner of the valley, considered to be the devil's gate, has the added advantage of natural protection from Mount Hiei.

Heian-Kyo was created with wide avenues, nine of which ran north–south, and eleven east–west, resulting in seventy-four blocks. In turn, these blocks were sub-divided into sixteen smaller blocks or *chō* – measuring approximately 120m (400ft) square. A *chō* was the standard size for aristocrats, although some families of high rank warranted two or four *chō*. The larger residences were mostly built in the northern and eastern parts of the city and, with them, the substantial gardens.

As well as encompassing earlier design concepts, many of these residences copied the natural features in and around Heian-Kyo. The mountains to three sides, with the open southerly aspect, accommodated the Chinese conceptual ideal of a comfortable armchair; mountains to the north forming the back of the chair and hills to the west and the east forming the arms. The armchair notion was also reflected in the layout of aristocratic estates. The main building included a large, south-facing hall – *shinden*. Corridors led to smaller, residential buildings to east and west, which, in turn, led southwards to pavilions, probably used for artistic performances or garden viewing. All the buildings looked out over the garden which lay to the south. Although somewhat

ABOVE: *Curved wooden bridge. Ritsurin Koen, Takamatsu.*

RIGHT: *Model of ancient Nara. Prefecture Office, Nara.*

smaller than their rural predecessors, the *shinden*-style gardens replicated the established style.

The Heian period was a time of cultural and political change in Japan. Significant among these was the continuing transition from Shintoism to Buddhism, with shifts in philosophical and spiritual attitudes.

The adoption of Buddhist philosophy in Japan began in the seventh century. With its structured teachings and disregard for status or clan, Buddhism afforded the Japanese the opportunity to move away from the feudal system and embrace the ideology that following Buddha's teachings gave the individual's life meaning and value. To impose this

RIGHT: *Palace complex in the Shinden style of the Heian era.*

BELOW: *Daibotsu-den hall of Tōdai-ji Temple. Nara.*

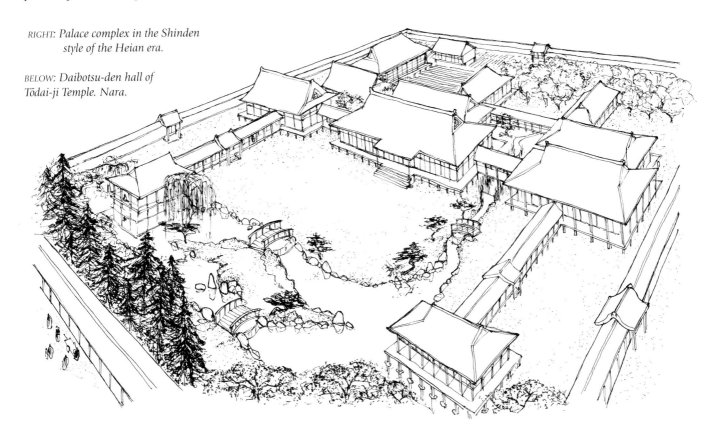

new ideology on the population the Emperor commissioned the building of temples, the most magnificent of which was the *Tōdai-ji*, housing the golden Buddha in its main hall – *Daibotsu-den*. The construction of the temple and its associated buildings happened before the Heian period, when temple complexes were built around large, open, inner courtyards, where religious ceremonies took place, but these were mostly devoid of gardens, whereas the temples of the Heian era began to be modelled on the *shinden*-style palace complexes of the time; the rectangular 'armchair' design enclosing a south-facing garden.

Kamakura Period (1185–1336)

Temple gardens became increasingly predominant during the twelfth century, probably attributable to the ever-growing awareness of the natural world and a deeply rooted desire to express this in artistic terms, together with the expanding association of the physical world with the spiritual beliefs of Buddhism. Added to which, the making of gardens was

Lower pond and strolling garden. 'The Moss Garden', kokedera, Saiho-ji Temple, Kyoto.

Early rock settings. Upper garden. 'The Moss Garden', kokedera, Saiho-ji Temple, Kyoto.

entrusted to priests who had the knowledge and understanding of Buddhist philosophy and rules. These priests were of low rank, similar to those who undertook the manual labour involved in working the land and were also usually of low social standing. This was soon to change.

Temple Pond Strolling Gardens

One of the most famous temple gardens was created during this time: the 'Moss Garden' – *kokedera* – of Saiho-ji Temple on the outskirts of Kyoto. The garden has two distinct areas; the lower is a pond strolling garden designed to be enjoyed on foot; the upper one is a *kare-sansui* garden set in a bed of moss. Unlike its successors, visitors stroll through all parts of the garden at Saiho-ji, contemplating it at leisure. This garden is, however, a landmark in the transition from the Heian pond-and-island-style 'paradise' garden to the more austere, dry landscape gardens. The rock settings include a turtle island in a 'sea' of moss, a flat-topped meditation stone – *zazen-seki*, and a dry waterfall – *kare-taki*, all of which provided inspiration for later gardens.

Muromachi Period (1336–1568)

The Muromachi period in Japan was a time of great turbulence, with social instability contrasting with artistic creativity and economic growth. Power struggles were rife, one of which, the Onin War, resulted in a large proportion of Kyoto being burnt to the ground. However, the shogunate and the temple hierarchies recognized and supported creative arts, including the design of gardens. Out of the ashes of instability and strife rose gardens for contemplation, in particular, those associated with Zen Buddhist temples.

The Increasing Spirituality of Strolling Gardens

The transition from 'strolling' gardens created solely for pleasurable pastimes, towards those with stronger spiritual significance continued through this period. In 1391 Shogun Ashikaga began conversion work on the *kitayama dono*, the 'Villa of the Northern Hills', which had been built in Kamakura times. He transformed it into a lavish residence in which to spend his retirement. After his death it became a Buddhist temple. The complex is popularly known as *Kinkaku-ji*, 'The Golden Temple', named after the

gilded, three-storeyed pavilion in Chinese style, magnificently isolated on an island. Other small islands in the surrounding pond feature crane and turtle islands.

In the late fifteenth century, Ashikaga Shogun Yoshimasa also devoted himself to constructing a retirement villa, known during his lifetime as *higashiyama dono*, the 'Villa of the Eastern Hills', due to its location on the eastern outskirts of Kyoto. After his death this became a Zen temple. Subsequently known as *Ginkaku-ji*, the 'Silver Temple', it had been intended to cover the main building in silver-gilt, but there is no evidence to suggest that this ever came to fruition.

The garden of the Silver Temple takes its inspiration from the garden of the *Saiho-ji* Temple, with a lower section for strolling around a pond with rocky islands, and an upper section of powerful rock settings in a moss bed. This garden contains what may be seen as some of the earliest representations of spiritual gardens created mainly from sand or gravel, and rocks. The ocean is represented by an area of

'The Golden Temple',
Kinkaku-ji. *Kyoto.*

white sand raked to suggest waves in the sea or moonbeams on the ocean, with the stylized Mount Fuji nearby.

'Kare-Sansui' *Gardens*

During this time the spreading Zen Buddhism in Japan had two branches: the *Rinzai* sect established by the priest Eisai, who believed in sudden enlightenment, whereas the *Sōtō* sect founded by the priest Dōgen sought gradual enlightenment. Both doctrines advocated meditation. Central to the practices of the *Sōtō* sect is seated meditation – *Zazen*, which concentrates on low breathing and the release of thoughts and emotions, enhancing the path to self-enlightenment. The emerging *kare-sansui* gardens increasingly became a vehicle not only for representing the world order, but also as a tool for relaxation and meditation.

In the middle ages, with increasing demands on the available land, sites of temple complexes began to change in form. The *shinden* style became more compressed, and the emphases on building and land usage changed. A large proportion of the temple sites became devoted to buildings for study and meditation, with ancillary buildings which housed the monks and kitchens in which to prepare food. Washing facilities were very spartan, often in the open air, sometimes using melting ice water for ablutions.

The wooden temples, in common with much traditional Japanese architecture, were raised above the ground, the substructure supported by stones to avoid the rotting of the timbers when the waters rose in the rainy seasons. Passage between buildings or rooms was usually via raised verandahs which overlooked the open spaces.

The main garden for contemplation was usually located to the south of the *hojo* or abbot's quarters. The viewing of the garden could be enjoyed either from within the building or by kneeling on the verandah. Typically the south wall of the building consisted of screens which folded back revealing the garden tableau. As the other three sides were in darkness, the large opening highlighted and framed the view, enhancing the tranquil ambience. One of the most famous rock and sand gardens can be viewed in this mind-focusing way. *Ryoan-ji*, the 'Temple of the Peaceful Dragon', is a *kare-sansui* in its purest form, devoid of significant plantings other than of moss discreetly surrounding the rock groupings. This masterpiece was built in 1488 after the original was burned in the Onin War. Studies have concluded that this garden was probably constructed by 'riverbank workers as gardeners' in conjunction with Zen monks.

The quality and uniqueness of *Ryoan-ji* can be attributed to its simplicity and large areas of emptiness. Scattered through the raked gravel are fifteen rocks, in the classic groupings of seven, five and three. There are many theories surrounding this garden: does it represent islands in the sea?

Raked white sand, with stylized Mt Fuji adjacent to 'The Silver Temple'. Kyoto.

Does it represent a mother tiger with her cubs crossing the ocean? Or is it solely a vehicle for peaceful meditation? Meditational techniques are intended to focus man's energies inwards towards his own consciousness. It is considered that this experience of 'nothingness' derived from personal insight could be facilitated by the garden at *Ryoan-ji* having no symbolism on which to dwell, thus allowing the emptying of the mind necessary to induce enlightenment.

Other *kare-sansui* gardens of the period allude to more specific images, and do include some tree or shrub plantings. The large temple complex of *Daitoku-ji*, to the north-west of Kyoto houses numerous buildings associated with a notable Buddhist monastery, including several sub-temples. The north garden at the *Ryogen-in* temple, *ryugintei*, is approximately 200m (660ft) square and is one of the most powerful surviving examples of Muromachi garden art. It is completely covered with moss, with a few trees at either end. A handsome, slanting rock, with supporting rocks, presides over many

ABOVE: *The rock garden at Ryoan-ji Temple on an autumnal afternoon. Kyoto.*

ABOVE RIGHT: *'Legend' of the rock garden at Ryoan-ji Temple, Kyoto.*

RIGHT: The North Garden, Ryūgintei *at Ryogen-in Temple,* Daitoku-ji *complex, Kyoto.*

smaller rocks; this rock has been variously interpreted as *Shumisen*, the Buddhist mountain at the centre of the world, a Buddhist triad or even a dry waterfall. It is unclear whether the covering moss was introduced during its building in the early sixteenth century or whether it has encroached on the white sand typical of the time.

In a corner of the *Daitoku-ji* complex is the *Daisen-in*, 'Great Hermit's Temple', which includes the exquisite, small-scale, dry gardens surrounding the abbot's quarters. Within these gardens are powerful rock settings and heavily manipulated plantings each element has a symbolic meaning and was designed to be studied from the north-east to the

Southern garden with Bodhi tree. Daisen-in Temple, Daitoku-ji *complex, Kyoto.*

BELOW LEFT: *'Ship at Sea' stone,* funa-shi. *Daisen-in Temple,* Daitoku-ji *complex, Kyoto.*

south-west, the whole representing the passage of human life. A 'river' of white gravel flows past the revered 'Mount Horai' and over a dam towards the west garden, eventually merging into an ocean of white gravel in the south garden in which stands a solitary bodhi tree, the tree under which it is reputed that Gautama Buddha, the father of Buddhism, achieved enlightenment. In the eastern garden is a renowned rock in the shape of a floating treasure boat, representing the wealth of experience that comes with age, a turtle stone attempts to swim against the current, underlining the futility of seeking to stem the flow of time.

Historically *Daisen-in* holds a unique place, linking for the first time themes of the Chinese Horai mountain myth with the austerity of a dry landscape garden. The garden scenes surround the temple, visitors enjoying the story they tell while passing through corridors and along verandah-style walkways.

Inspiration for the dry gardens was also borrowed from black and white ink-wash paintings. The Chinese priests who migrated to Japan in the twelfth century brought with them artistic prowess, including the drawing of images of their world. Initially the monochromatic ink paintings were of spiritual subjects such as famous Zen priests or Buddhas in a landscape setting. Sesshū Tōyō, a Japanese scholar of the fifteenth century, broke away from traditional subject matter, using the medium purely to express aesthetic scenes which were reinterpreted in garden settings. The likenesses were often painted on sliding screens or panels within temples and other buildings, many of which survive to this day. Translating these images into garden settings with the use of dark rocks, white sand and dark green plantings is a trademark of the Muromachi period.

Momoyama Period (1568–1603)

Daimyo Castle Gardens

Throughout the Momoyama period, the building of pond gardens continued. Gardens of the early Momoyama period are different from those of the preceding Muromachi stereotype. Designs became more complex, with undulating pond margins giving rise to peninsulas and bays. The ruling class of the day, the daimyo lords, wanted to show off their creative skills and imported ever larger rocks to incorporate into their gardens. It is possible that the skills needed to handle these weighty stones were developed during the construction of the massive ramparts protecting the daimyo castles.

The castles, surrounded by townships, became the centres of culture in which the arts flourished and spread throughout the country. As the new leaders in artistic endeavour, the palaces of the daimyo superseded the aristocratic residences and pure land temples of the Heian period and the shogunal villa retreats and Zen temples of the Muromachi era.

Although these early Momoyama pond gardens were still used for strolling through, the primary aim was to provide a scene to be viewed from the *shoin*, a contemporary style of architecture which included a desk – *tsuke-shoin*, built into an alcove. The desk was used for reading and writing and, significantly, looked out over the garden.

Tea Gardens

In contrast during this period, another important and familiar garden type was developed and became highly sophisticated: the tea garden. Japanese history, art and culture are represented in the tea ceremony – *cha-no-yu* or *sado* – a symphony of intricate movements which combine with the total environment to create a spiritual and artistic experience.

In the twelfth century, Eisai Zenshi, a Japanese Zen pioneer, encouraged tea drinking to prolong life and promote a healthy constitution. A sixteenth-century tea master, Murato Shuko, isolated tea-taking from the usual environment of residences or temples and raised it to an art form inspiring tea houses – *sōan*. Tea-taking began to develop as a spiritual pursuit. The tea ceremony is still socially recognized as a vehicle for today's busy family to transport the senses into a state of relaxation, alertness and receptiveness in order to appreciate non-material values.

Sen-no-Rikyu, another renowned sixteenth-century tea master, elevated the tea ceremony from a simple pastime to a 'way of truth'. He also pioneered the concept of the path to the tea house being a course of meditation and inspiration for peace, deriving the customary tea garden name – *roji* – dewy path. The early tea houses were intended to resemble the retreat of a hermit; they were small, detached huts in the back gardens of rather cramped town houses. Walking from the residence to the tea house via the *roji* is evocative of a journey from the urban environment through the woods to the hermitage in the mountains, preparing the mind, body and spirit for the ceremony.

Furuta Oribe, who followed Rikyu as an influential tea master, felt that Rikyu's gardens were too rustic and therefore introduced more formality by placing trees and stones in structured and more pleasing positions. He divided gardens with bamboo fences of varying designs and small gates which mark transitions and make punctuations, reawaking spiritual awareness and directing changes in mood. Oribe was also the designer of a lantern style which bears his name.

Before the arrival of the guests the tea master will have cleaned the tea house and the garden. Adjacent to the tea

ABOVE: Roji, *the path to the tea house.*
Omote Senke School of Tea, Kyoto.

RIGHT: *Transitional gateway.*
Omote Senke School of Tea, Kyoto.

BELOW: *'Oribe' lantern and 'well head'.*
Private garden, Kyoto.

house is a pit for garden litter indicating cleanliness. The garden will be sprinkled with water, another sign of cleanliness, as well as hinting at a dewy morning in the hills. On entering the garden and becoming physically and psychologically detached from the outside world, guests move into a reception or waiting area, where they rest, usually seated on a covered bench, until called for by the host.

At the behest of the host or hostess, guests proceed through the outer garden towards the inner garden, passing through another gateway. At Omote Senke, the headquarters of a famous school of tea in Kyoto, this gate, *naka-kuguri*, involves a crawl through a structure which makes guests conscious of their body and is a humbling experience necessary for progression to the tea room. Latticed bamboo gates – *agesudo* – are frequently used for the transition points. They are less structured and more manageable than wooden gates, and are often held open with a stick, allowing guests to pass unhindered.

En route there will be a well, either real or representational, implying that fresh water is available for the tea making and for personal cleansing. On approaching the tea house, guests cleanse themselves at a stone water basin set so that, again, one has to stoop to it; by stooping all are made equal. A ladle, usually made of bamboo, is provided for guests to use. Traditionally, raised stepping stones form the path itself, *tobi-ishi*, a feature which may have originated to avoid numerous feet crushing the carpeting mosses and to preserve the ladies' delicate silk kimonos. They also serve to focus attention on each footfall and to make participants aware of the soles of their feet. In front of the tea house will be one or several higher stones, elevating guests to a position

ABOVE: Litter pit adjacent to tea house. Isui-en, Nara.

RIGHT: Waiting bench. Isui-en, Nara.

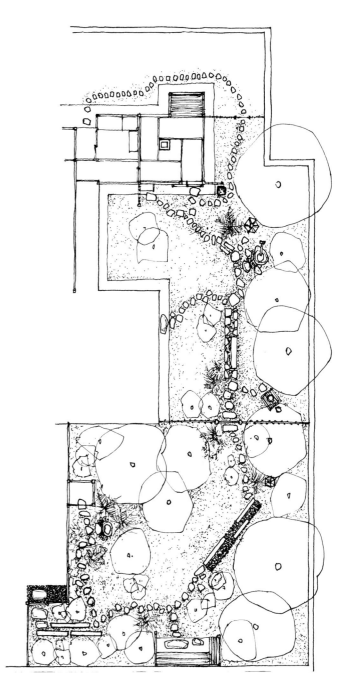

ABOVE:
Kasuga-*style lantern.*
Takamatsu Castle garden, Takamatsu.

OPPOSITE PAGE:
TOP LEFT: Naka-kuguri.
Omote Senke School of Tea, Kyoto.

TOP RIGHT: Raised gateway – *agesudo.*
Omote Senke School of Tea, Kyoto.

BOTTOM LEFT: Stone water-basin grouping.
Private garden, Kyoto.

BOTTOM RIGHT: Entrance to the Tea House, nijiri-guchi.
Omote Senke School of Tea, Kyoto.

Plan of tea garden.

from which they can enter the tea room through a small door – *nijiri-guchi*, designed so that samurai warriors could not pass through while wearing a sword. Storage places for swords would be provided.

Tea ceremonies were and are performed at various times throughout the day, sometimes after darkness has fallen. As it was necessary to provide light for visitors to traverse the garden safely, the use of carved granite lanterns at strategic points was adopted. Lanterns had long been used to provide light in temple complexes. Variations on the established designs became commonplace, with the developing of new styles more specifically created for use in *roji*.

Entrance to the Tea House, nijiri-guchi.
Kasa-tei, Kodai-ji, Kyoto.

Early Edo Period (1603–88)

Although a relatively short period in history, the Early Edo era saw the construction of many significant gardens. It was a time of peace and increasing insularity during which, once again, Chinese spiritual influences came to the fore. With a decline in Buddhism, Confucian beliefs were revived, as they allowed the ruling classes more power. The concept of human order based on loyalty, government and intellectual orthodoxy, together with the Chinese ideal of bureaucratic civil rule were useful tools for the Tokugawa shogunate and the provincial daimyo overlords.

Further Developments in Daimyo Castle Garden Design

With peace and stability came a time during which energies could be concentrated on artistic achievement, including the construction of large gardens which would not become the victims of social unrest and destruction. The daimyo, whose power was restricted by the shogunate, vied with each other through the accumulation of material possessions and artistic expression.

Gardens, once again, became places to entertain guests of the daimyo, who were the political leaders in charge of a province. Even though it was obligatory for the daimyo to be in the capital city Edo – modern-day Tokyo – for half the year, it was still a matter of station and expression of wealth to maintain a provincial castle and associated garden. When the shogun or noble princes were travelling around the country, the daimyo estates provided resting places for the nobles and their entourages.

Imperial Palace and Villa Gardens

Coincident with the creation of castle gardens in the early seventeenth century, was the commissioning of gardens associated with imperial palaces and villas within townships and in more rural locations. In Kyoto, the site of the Imperial Palace and its grounds occupies a significant area of the city and survives today. Within the grounds, surrounded by clay-tiled, mud walls, is the garden of Sento Gosho – the palace for ex-emperors, which was begun by the Tokugawa

Shogunate in 1627, housing two ponds with a series of bridges of different styles, including one that was covered; others were made of stone, wooden planks or logs. Tea pavilions were built on the banks of the ponds, with associated stone groupings. Following fires in 1660 and 1673 which destroyed the buildings, rebuilding took place, including the remodelling of the garden, since which time it has gone through many changes in design to become the tranquil garden which can be enjoyed into the present century.

Strolling gardens of the Edo period continued to move away from symbolism based on various belief systems and expanded on earlier ideas of reproducing scenes from the natural world. At this time was built one of the rural retreats of the imperial family to the south of Kyoto near the Katsura River. The villa and garden of Katsura Rikyu were commissioned by Prince Toshihito, who was deeply impressed by a peninsula on the north coast of Japan called *Ama-no-hashidate* – 'Bridge to Heaven'. It is reputed to have been so named because of the pine trees which grow naturally along the peninsula. If an onlooker were to observe this combination of horizontal land form with vertical tree form

RIGHT: Entrance to garden.
Sento Gosho, Kyoto.

BELOW: Stone bridge.
Sento Gosho, Kyoto.

'Ama-no-Hashidate'.
Katsura rikyu, Kyoto.

BELOW: Kare-sansui *garden with 'Crane' and 'Turtle' islands. Manshu-in, Kyoto.*

upside down, it could be considered to resemble a bridge built on stilts. Toshihito wanted a representation of this scene; the stone peninsula with granite 'lighthouse' protruding into the pond at Katsura Rikyu has become one of the most famous features of any garden and has been frequently reinterpreted over the centuries.

During the Edo period, other design influences persisted, including the desire to view gardens by boat, from vantage points within buildings or on foot. The meandering paths in the garden of Katsura Rikyu were modelled on the *roji* paths, and link several buildings, including a number of tea arbours.

Further Developments in Kare-Sansui *Gardens*

Other design styles became reinterpreted through the Edo periods, in particular the dry landscape gardens, which bore little resemblance to those of earlier periods. Plantings became more prolific and, together with stone groupings, took on greater significance, with a return to symbolic representations of myths, legends and spiritual beliefs.

The garden at Manshu-in, reputed to have been built in the mid seventeenth century, has a free-flowing form, depicting a natural landscape incorporating the Mount Horai theme – 'turtle' and 'crane' islands being clearly depicted by unusual rock and plant groupings. Following the example of Momoyama gardens, the garden at Manshu-in is designed to be viewed from the *shoin*, from where all the traditional attributes of a dry landscape garden are revealed.

Middle and Later Edo Periods (1688–1868)

Less Formal Kare-Sansui

With subtle changes, the design of dry landscape gardens continued into the middle and the later Edo periods. In many instances, although still associated with temples, the emphasis on contemplation and symbolism became diluted, and more naturalistic compositions were created in which the designers' artistry could be admired in less formal settings.

The garden at the Shoden-ji Temple skilfully captures this trend, being designed to be viewed from a fixed point looking over an expanse of raked white gravel in the foreground. In the middle ground are fifteen clipped azaleas in a seven, five and three formation, following the tradition of earlier gardens such as Ryoan-ji. The azaleas, which are pruned to resemble rock groupings, give a softer, more feminine, feel to the garden.

A white, tile-topped, mud wall enfolds the garden over which can be seen trees and bamboos growing in their natural habitat and framed in the far distance can be seen the peak of Mount Hiei. The surrounding landscape and mountain view, although not within the boundaries of the garden, become an integral part of the whole. This technique of extending the garden scene into the distance is a particular skill of Japanese garden designers, referred to as *shakkei* or borrowed view.

ABOVE: Granite water basin and 'path through the country'. Katsura rikyu, Kyoto.

RIGHT: Pathway climbing yuishi-san. Koraku-en, Okayama.

'Natural' Strolling Gardens

Meanwhile the established trends continued in the design and functions of gardens for strolling around, with a continuing emphasis on recreational pursuits rather than symbolism and meditation. Many of the large gardens were developed over several generations by their daimyo owners. Each designer incorporated new ideas, at the same time respecting previous works and maintaining harmony throughout.

Several of the gardens reputed to be the most beautiful in Japan were developed during this period. The trend of representing 'natural' scenes, either real or imagined, continued; however, their appearance overall was less formal than in earlier periods. The creation of artificial hills was popularized, with gentle contours and grass-covered slopes. Water continued to provide the central core to strolling gardens. Ponds with gradually sloping banks superseded the earlier fashions for imposing rock edgings and artificial beaches, and winding streams became wider and, in addition to bridges, crossings were formed from large, flat stepping stones – *sawatari-ishi*.

Koraku-en in Okayama is a fine example of a garden evolving over a long period from the mid seventeenth century to the late nineteenth, when it was opened as a public park. Within the garden a winding stream links several ponds which, in turn, contain small islands. Earth which had been excavated for creating the ponds and artificial rivers was used to build nearby 'hillsides', a technique still practised today. Within Koraku-en garden is such an artificial mountain – *yuishin-san*, 'sole heart mountain' – which may be climbed via gently sloping paths, passing beside heavily clipped azaleas which hint at hillside rocks. At an elevated resting place visitors can overlook the garden and from this viewpoint may be seen one of the tea arbours – *ryuten-tei*, 'teahouse by the stream'. Of a totally different style to the winding streams of Heian times, a structured stream with stepping stones passes through a corner of the building in which the 'Feast by the Winding Stream' takes place.

Within the garden of Koraku-en is another innovation, a small plantation of *Camellia thea*, the plant used to make the green tea prepared in tea ceremonies, which introduces the representation of everyday activities into the garden story. The atmosphere of Koraku-en and other similar gardens of the later Edo periods, is of lightness and cheerfulness, in contrast to gardens of the Momoyama era which were more powerful and subdued.

Modern Era

Meiji Period (1868–1912)

Towards the end of the nineteenth century, Japanese isolationism ceased with the signing of a friendship treaty between Japan and the USA, which was given permission to establish consular offices in Japan. This was seen by many as proof that the shogunate were no longer powerful

ABOVE: *'Tea Plantation'. Koraku-en, Okayama.*

LEFT: Kare-sansui *garden with clipped azaleas and* shakkei *with Mt Hiei in background. Shoden-ji, Kyoto.*

enough to keep outsiders away, and in 1866 the emperor regained power. The samurai and daimyo classes were abolished and Western civilization began to be adopted.

In the Meiji era, with the modernization resulting from exposure to the West, the open spaces available for creating gardens broadened from the traditional shrine, temple, castle and residential gardens to include open spaces associated with new buildings such as offices, schools, hotels and railway stations.

CHANGING STYLES FOR DOMESTIC GARDENS

During the Meiji era, the style of gardens adjoining private residences underwent subtle changes. New layouts for pond gardens were developed. One of the new styles was narrow at the ends and broader in the middle, a fine example of which is at the villa of Murin-an at the foothills of Kyoto's eastern mountain range, built for Prince Aritomo Yamagata and completed in 1896. At the eastern end of the garden is a naturalistic waterfall fed from Lake Biwa lying to the north-east; the waterfall tumbles into a stream which gently flows through two ponds and finally joins a second stream. The calming atmosphere of the garden is engendered by horizontal rock placings, meandering across a large area of lawn and moss. The garden and *shakkei* of the hills beyond may either be contemplated from the tea house or enjoyed on foot.

Similarly, the garden of Isui-en in Nara, completed in 1890, was designed for strolling through while enjoying the distant *shakkei* which includes views of Nara's three famous mountains, as well as the upper part of the Todaiji Temple housing the great golden Buddha. The naturalistic waterfall flows into a stream across which millstone stepping stones lead to a central island. The stream is bordered by azaleas clipped to represent boulders, a technique typical of the Meiji era. A small, rustic tea arbour and garden contrast with the larger strolling garden.

Showa Period (1926–89)

Historically, the craft of designing gardens was hereditary, passed through the generations from father to son or to son-in-law. With the proliferation of new buildings and exposure to Western culture, different design skills were required, often drawing on the knowledge of architects and garden historians who worked in co-operation with the old-fashioned, 'hands-on' gardeners, whose practical experience was invaluable.

The garden of Murin-an with shakkei *beyond. Murin-an, Kyoto.*

View across pond with shakkei *beyond. Isui-en, Nara.*

MODERN INTERPRETATIONS
OF TRADITIONAL DESIGNS

During this time, the desire for naturalistic compositions did little to promote the creation of *kare-sansui* dry gardens with their contrived abstraction and symbolism. However, with the advent of the Showa period, *kare-sansui* gardens experienced a resurgence. Partly responsible for this was the creation of many new, and the restoration of some older, temple gardens, and partly too the foresight and creativity of the garden artist and historian Mirei Shigemori.

One of Shigemori's most innovative projects was the redesigning of gardens surrounding the new buildings at Tofuki-ji Temple in eastern Kyoto. A fire in 1880 had destroyed the abbot's quarters and other temple buildings. Rebuilding began in 1889. In 1940 Shigemori began designing the four gardens which surround the temple buildings. The south garden accommodates the concept of 'old' and 'new' mountains of the east and the west, set in silver sand against a backdrop of whitewashed mud walls ornately tiled with grey clay tiles, and with a magnificent, central, traditional gateway.

The other three gardens express a more modern approach to the design of *kare-sansui* gardens. In the eastern garden are set seven round stones of differing height representing the main stars of the 'Great Bear in Heaven'. The stones were originally the foundation stones for the piers of an earlier river bridge. In the west and the north garden geometric shapes are interspersed with plantings. The west garden has

ABOVE: *'Great Bear Garden'.*
Tofuku-ji Temple, Kyoto.

LEFT: *West Garden.*
Tofuku-ji Temple, Kyoto.

clipped Satsuki azaleas in a chequerboard pattern, alternating with white sand imitating '*seiden*', a Chinese way of dividing land. In contrast, the north garden contains irregularly placed stepping stones embedded in moss and sand. All four gardens are to be viewed from the building and physically entered only by those who tend to the plantings and maintain the raked gravel in pristine condition.

Another innovative creation of Mirei Shigemori is the 'Showa New Garden' of the Matsuo Grand Shrine, located at the foot of a verdant hill on the west side of Kyoto. This garden consists of three landscape gardens with an abundance of stones, some of which festoon the bamboo-clad hillside and represent the deities. Stonework also abounds in the pond garden, which is very stylized, with hard edges and mirror-smooth water. A newly-painted shrine building contrasts with the monochromatic theme of this part of the garden.

LEFT: *North Garden.*
Tofuku-ji Temple, Kyoto.

BELOW: *Pond Garden.*
Matsuo shrine, Kyoto.

ABOVE: *Roof garden.*
Kyoto Station.

Stepped waterfalls.
Suzaku no Niwa, Kyoto.

Heisei Period (1989–)

Towards the end of the last century, many of the established stroll gardens associated with shrines, temples, castles and palaces were opened to the public.

GARDENS WITH A STORY TO TELL

At the same time, new gardens were created for public enjoyment. Some of the recent creations employ modern techniques while retaining distinctive Japanese design styles and also telling a story of Japanese life and traditions. In 1994, to celebrate the 1,200th anniversary of the foundation of Kyoto, in addition to the restoration of some important shrines and gardens, a commemorative park and garden were constructed on reclaimed land once occupied by a railway freight depot. Umekoji Park was not in an ideal environment for creating a flourishing garden, being bordered by a railway line, commercial buildings and apartment houses, but within the park, built on only 0.9ha (2.2 acres) of land is *suzaku no Niwa* – the Garden of the

Suzaku. The aims of the design were to create a new style that matched community life in modern Kyoto and at the same time moved on from imitating traditional gardens. Represented in the garden is a mountain stream with autumnal tints – *momiji-dani* – with elevated walkway through the tree canopy. The 'landscape' then opens into a depiction of rice paddies, leading to fields beside a river or road. The water-surface mirror – *mizukagami* – is based on the art of Ogata Korin, a painter of the Edo period, which attempts to convey the unexpectedness of an unreal landscape. The smooth water is punctuated by stepped, gentle waterfalls designed in a way very different from the traditional waterfalls tumbling through natural rocks.

The modern railway system in Japan is held in high regard, with enormous investment in new stations. The recently completed main station in Kyoto is a vast complex of platforms, restaurants, department stores, hotels and a theatre. But the garden tradition is not forgotten: in the basement is a contemporary 'shishi-odoshi', a reminder of the deer scarers of yesteryear. On the roof, high above the city, are simple geometric planters, each housing a single tree.

3

Design Elements

The choice and arrangement of materials in Japanese gardens instantly gives them a distinctive air. An atmosphere is frequently set before one enters the main garden by creating a change in mood and a transition from the everyday street scene to the tranquillity of the garden. These transitions are often in the form of a pavement or pathway, sometimes leading to an entrance way, sometimes traversing a front garden.

Pavements and Pathways

Pavements have been associated for centuries with the approaches to shrine and temple gardens, as well as tea gardens. More recently, pavements of different styles have been installed at the approaches to private gardens.

The Western interpretation of the word 'pavement' is somewhat different from the Japanese usage. Early pavements in Japan were constructed from natural stone, usually hand selected for colour and shape. Varying patterns in laying the stones developed, some random, others more structured. Where one type of stone was used the pavement edges may have been straight with the main body being random, or the whole pavement may have been more random in layout with uneven edges. Random, natural stones which have been smoothed by tumbling through rivers and over waterfalls hint at a rural or rustic environment, but, with the ability to cut the hard granite into geometric shapes, pavements could be constructed from larger units with more structured finishes. Imaginative patterns were introduced which included the laying of oblong slabs lengthwise to give a uniform footfall, or the skilful fitting together of differently sized rectangles of hewn granite. If there needs to be

OPPOSITE PAGE:
Yukimi-gata *beside tea house.*
Kenrokuen, Kanazawa.

THIS PAGE:
Random stone pavement.
Private garden, Kyoto.

Gyo pavement.
Katsura Rikyu, Kyoto.

Granite slab and gravel path.
Byodo-in, Uji.

a change of direction in a path this is achieved by a junction which is not a right angle. A geometric layout suggests a more urban and formal situation.

A combination of natural stones forming smaller units and cut rectangular pieces were and are used to create interesting pathways. Variations include what is known as the *gyō* style, where geometric shapes are interspersed with random, natural shapes.

The pavements approaching some shrines and temples are constructed in another pleasing combination, with straight-cut, narrow edgings between which square-cut pieces are set in a diamond formation, the gaps being filled with either loose aggregate or natural pebbles.

All these techniques may be used in Western gardens. To achieve an authentic Japanese style, the selection of materials is important. Much of the stone intrinsic to Japan is hard granite, in varying shades of grey. However, in the West granite is

not always available, is heavy to handle, difficult to cut and may be priced above the budget for a particular job. With the proliferation of manufactured materials and imports from around the world it is possible to source more manageable materials; manufactured imitations of granite in shades of grey with either smooth or rough finishes are readily available. Where pavements are used by pedestrians, it is important that the surface of the stones should not become slippery when wet; stone with rough surfaces is the safest. Natural stone is also available in uniform sizes, thinly cut, and much more manageable. The substitutes are ideal for a modern look; however, they do not replace the might of more substantial pieces of granite. Sometimes it is possible to find granite in reclamation yards or stone merchants.

Where a pavement or pathway reaches the entrance to a garden there will be a threshold, usually with a change of materials which focuses the mind of the visitor. Traditionally,

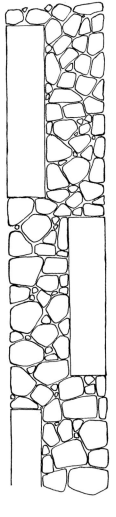

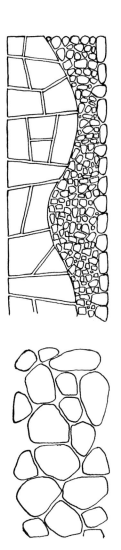

ABOVE: *Pavement formations.*

ABOVE RIGHT: *Pre-cut granite paving slabs. Exhibition garden, Birmingham, England.*

RIGHT: *Gateway and threshold. Nomura Samurai house, Kanazawa.*

thresholds have been of large, natural stones which, yet again, make the visitor aware of the changing mood.

Once inside the garden, the style of the pathways changes. The combinations of natural and cut stone typically become less formal and more flowing. It may still be that straight-sided pathways are constructed; the junctions may take the form of one part of the path ending abruptly, while another begins to the side of it, thereby reducing the effect of perspective and demanding the attention of pedestrians to negotiate the changing routes. A pathway may also end abruptly, directing the visitor on to stepping stones, where mood and pace change again.

Installation of Pavements and Pathways

There are several methods of installing pavements and pathways, the choice of which depends on the site, the structure of the soil or subsoil and the materials to be used. The priority is to ensure that the finished work will be safe for pedestrians. On a level site where the soil is stable, the most straightforward approach is to reduce the level of the ground to accommodate the depth of the chosen materials, plus allowing a depth for a base which may be compacted scalpings to a depth of 100mm (4in) topped with coarse sand. The natural soil is levelled and firmed, followed by the base layer and, finally, the paving material. This method is particularly suitable where the materials are of uniform depth, such as manufactured slabs and tiles, or evenly cut natural stone. The stone may be closely abutted or, where appropriate, gaps can be left which are filled with ground-cover plants, traditionally moss but more recently *Ophiopogon japonicus* 'Tamaryu' 'Dragon's whiskers', which more successfully withstands harsh treatment and drought.

When using randomly-shaped, natural stone and/or pebbles, which may be of varying thickness, it is preferable to set the materials in concrete. Reduce the ground level to below the finished surface level, taking into account the depth of the concrete base, 75mm (3in), plus the depth of the thickest stone. Once the base had dried, more wet concrete is applied, in which the stones are set; it is at this stage that adjustment may be made for different thicknesses, checking the finished levels. When constructing pavements in this way, it is necessary to consider drainage. If the site is adjacent to an area which will drain naturally, providing a slight gradient away from any building may suffice. In circumstances where the paved area is of considerable size, it may be advisable to install a drainage system.

Changing moods.
Jonangu-ji Temple, Kyoto.

Laying cut granite path. Private garden, Dorset, England.

Laying random stone pavement.
Private garden, Dorset, England.

BELOW: Stepping stones layout.

Stepping Stones – *tobi ishi*

Stepping stones gained prominence in the Momoyama period when *roji* gardens were developed as a route to guide visitors towards the tea house. Later, in the Edo period, the use of stepping stones and their placing is a ruse by which the designer can direct the visitors' gaze towards particular features, either within the garden or in the borrowed scenery (*shakkei*).

Installing Stepping Stones

The use of medium-sized natural stones of 300–400mm (12–16in) is the time-honoured choice. Ideally, the stones should be almost flat and without a depression in their surface so that water cannot collect there and become slippery. Stepping stones should be at least 100mm (4in) thick so that, when set, they will be raised above the finished surface level. Stones are laid in a meandering fashion, with the longer axis perpendicular to the desired route. As the path twists and turns so do the stone placings. Stones are placed at spacings of 100 to 150mm (4–6in). The narrower gaps being necessary for the enforced limited pace of kimono-clad ladies. Narrow and irregular spacings slow the pace of pedestrians, whereas slightly wider and uniform spacings allow a faster passage. When using naturally weathered stones, their juxtapositioning needs careful planning: those with flat or nearly flat sides adjacent to one another and those with a convexity next to those with a concavity. A skilled designer achieves this instinctively, preferably having had the opportunity to

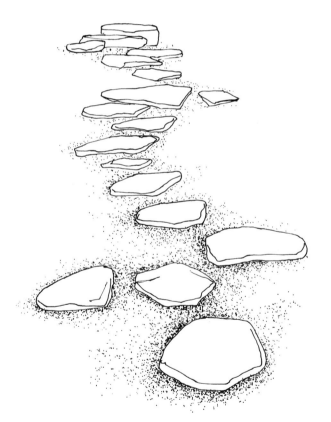

choose stones for their individual qualities beforehand. If there is a divergence in the path, a large, pivotal stone is set at the junction. Subdued, natural colours are preferred, but there may be slight variations in texture. Where possible, it is preferable to use natural stone, either in free-form or cut.

Again, in the West, this may be difficult to find or too highly priced for the budget. Pre-cast substitutes are available in appropriate sizes and colours. Some manufacturers offer a variety of shapes which can be arranged randomly.

Stepping stones may also be of cut stone, usually squares, which may be laid diagonally, forming diamonds or, alternatively, diagonally plus 'square-on', breaking the uniformity. Sometimes millstones are used to make stepping stone paths; they may either be reclaimed or newly crafted.

In a modern Japanese-style garden stepping stones may meander across an expanse of grass or some other ground-cover plant. When deciding on the finished pattern, the stones are laid on the surface and adjusted to achieve the required effect. Outlines of the stones are then scribed on the ground and holes dug to a depth such that the stones will be approximately 50mm (2in) above ground level. Having placed each stone in its hole and adjusted the height, pack soil or pebbles around it, ensuring that it is firm. Stepping stones that are not partly buried, need to be firmly set on concrete bases, such as those incorporated into a pavement adjacent to a building or when crossing a dry stone garden.

Where stepping stones lead to an entrance to a building, the nearer the entrance, the larger should be the stones. If the building is raised above the ground, as in traditional Japanese architecture, the stones nearest the house will be stepped in height, with the deepest immediately in front of the doorway. If the building is more or less level with the garden, larger stones may still be installed nearer the doorway, but at approximately the same level as in the main path. In Japan it is customary for all to remove their outdoor shoes before entering a building, particularly where there are delicate mats (*tatami*) or wooden floors, and to replace them with slippers. The large

ABOVE: Installing natural stone tobi-ishi. *Private garden, Dorset, England.*

RIGHT: Laying pre-cast stepping stones. School courtyard garden, Hampshire, England.

stone nearest the doorway (*kutsunugi-ishi*, shoe-removing stone) is a repository for footwear.

Pavements Next to Buildings

The outside space which interfaces with the building and forms a transition between the two has customarily been paved and is another opportunity for designers to be creative, matching the choice of materials with the style of house. Cobblestones can create a rustic feel, whereas larger pieces give a more formal appearance. Random pieces of natural stone may be laid like crazy paving; however, the mortar is recessed below the level of the stone and is usually of a complementary colour. A popular stone is *tanba-ishi*, with a browner colour than is usually seen in Japanese gardens, and which is mined in Kameoka, near to Kyoto. In the West an excellent substitute is natural Yorkstone, particularly if it is reclaimed and has weathered and darkened.

If an even more formal and uniform finish is required, dark grey or black stone is often used, cut into square 'tile'-sized units of 150 to 250mm (6–10in), set in a diamond formation. If a dense natural stone is not available, dark grey or black floor tiles are equally as effective, sometimes made from cut slate or dark sandstone, sometimes from glazed clay. Unless pedestrians avoid this surface by walking on inset stepping stones, it is important to ensure that the material does not become slippery when wet.

If there is a roof overhanging from the building, the *noki-iuchi* ('inside the eaves') pavement is usually bordered by a

Tobi-ishi *and* kutsunugi-ishi. *Entrance to tea house, Hakusasonō garden, Kyoto.*

Reclaimed Yorkstone pavement and weathered Purbeck stone kutsunugi-ishi. *Private garden, Dorset, England.*

Pavings and drainage channels.
Daitoku-ji *Temple complex, Kyoto.*

Offloading 'maxi' bag of pearly quartz for
kare-sansui. *Private garden, Dorset, England.*

pebble-filled channel to drain away rain which falls from the eaves when there is no guttering.

Gravels

The use of gravels in gardens began modestly in the Nara period and reached the zenith of popularity from the Muromachi period onwards, particularly for use in *kare-sansui* gardens. An off-white gravel produced in Kita-Shirakawa, near Kyoto, was one of the first to be used to depict water in these gardens. Contrary to popular belief, stark white gravels, such as white marble, are not suitable owing to their distracting brightness. Off-white, silver-grey and beige gravels are the most favoured. Silver-grey material was also collected from the Shirakawa district, derived from a soft granite

which had weathered to form a fine gravel. From the Mie area comes an unusually soft, brownish granite, crushed to make gravel, which darkens when wet, and popularly used in modern dry gardens.

In the West variously sourced grits and gravels are available in a choice of colours, either in manageable prepacks or bulk bags holding approximately a tonne.

Pebbles

In addition to gravels, pebbles, cobbles and other naturally formed stones are commonly used in Japanese-style gardens. Water-tumbled cobblestones, measuring about 100–150mm (4–6in) in diameter have popularly been gathered and used in gardens as edging stones, as well as integral parts of pavements.

ABOVE: Pebble 'beach' and stepping stones. Kyoto garden, Holland Park, London, England.

RIGHT: 'Paddlestone' stream. Private garden, Berkshire, England.

They are also used to recreate stone beaches either on river banks or lake shorelines, and to form stone peninsulas.

Of similar size, but flatter than cobbles, are the materials referred to as 'paddlestones'. These are typically pieces of dark grey granite or slate which have fallen from larger formations, usually as a result of weathering, and have subsequently been tossed about in fast running rivers or back and forth along the seashore, resulting in smooth surfaces and rounded edges. Where they are available in sufficient quantities, they have been used in Japan to create the impression of flowing water, each stone being carefully selected and laid in a specific relationship to its neighbours, thus giving the appearance of a river. These flat stones may also be used in conjunction with rounder ones to represent a more natural dry river bed.

In the West paddlestones can sometimes be obtained in their natural state, but, because of consumer demand and international environmental regulations, they are becoming less readily available, and consequently suppliers are now using rough-sided fragments which are dry tumbled in rotating drums to soften their edges. Although effective, this process does scar the surface, resulting in whitish patches when the stones are dry. A recently developed method of artificially weathering stones is to tumble them in a mixture of sand and gravel, which more closely mimics natural processes.

Smaller pebbles are also used when building dry water-falls (*kare-taki*), giving the impression of water flowing over rocks and through canyons. Substantial standing rocks form the basis of *kare-taki*, which will be described more fully in Chapter 6.

Stone Groupings

Stone arrangements are greatly cherished in Japanese gardens. The chosen stones are usually granite, which is widespread, weathers fast and is best suited for lower stones; andesite, a type of volcanic rock that is formed as lava cools and, due to its weather-resistant qualities, retains sharper edges and is ideal for rock groupings, and the highly treasured blue stone, which is formed from chlorite schist or crystalline schist obtained from several areas in Japan and has strongly veined markings and is perfectly suited for rock arrangements designed to resemble ink paintings.

Selecting Rocks

There are some guidelines in selecting garden rocks. For a particular grouping, obtain rocks from the same source to enhance the impression of a natural scene. Rocks of different colours and types will look overly contrived. Although rocks come alive when wet, they are best chosen when dry.

It is important to study the shape and structure of each rock and to envisage them in the garden setting.

Depending on the size and the style of the garden, rocks are used in many ways, the placing of which is clearly described in *The Sakuteiki*, the twelfth-century manuscript on garden design, now available in English translation (*see* Bibliography). *The Sakuteiki* is also cautionary about how *not* to place stones, such as 'placing sideways the stone which was originally set vertically, or setting up vertically the stone which was originally laid sideways is taboo', or 'do not place stone where rainwater from the house eaves drops on it. A person getting the spray of such raindrops would contract bad skin diseases because of the poisonous effect of water which comes down from the cypress-bark roofing and hits that stone.' There are also many instructions about where to place stones and which way they should face; disobeying these instructions can bring misfortune to the home-owner.

Installing Rocks

Having chosen the stones at the quarry or the stone merchants, the skilled designer knows where each will be placed, and the site needs to be prepared for them beforehand. The largest stone in a grouping will be set first, followed in sequence down to the smallest. To be visually and physically stable, a large proportion of each stone is buried beneath the surface and set firmly, preferably in concrete. When it is not possible to achieve a perfect balance, plantings between the stones can regain the desired effect. Whether

Rock and stone store. Landscape gardening company, Kyoto.

Setting largest stone of sanzon-seki *grouping.*
Private garden, Dorset, England.

Traditional stone-based wall, topped with 'mud'
wall and clay tiles. Private house, Kyoto.

stones are used to represent the Buddhist triad, to form 'crane' and 'turtle' islands, to create the main structure of dry waterfalls or to surround ponds, the principles of choice and installation remain the same.

Walls

Rock and Mud Walls

Substantial rocks have traditionally been used to build the base for perimeter walls. Natural stone walls are sometimes topped with mud walls, which, in turn, may be capped with distinctive clay tiles, shingles or even pointed bamboo used as a deterrent to intruders. Low stone walls may be used to retain soil banks into which hedges are planted or as the base for bamboo fences.

Mud walls have been familiar on the Japanese street scene for centuries, often as boundaries for temple complexes or to enclose the gardens of wealthy merchants or warriors. Intricately designed and precisely crafted grey clay tiles usually forming the capping. Equally as impressive, but less durable, are the cappings created from layers of cedarwood shingles, a highly labour-intensive technique.

To recreate similar walls in the West is a challenge to the designer and to the finances of the client. However, when the circumstances are right, the inclusion of such a wall gives a Japanese-style garden added authenticity. The wall itself can be constructed from concrete blocks or bricks, which are rendered and colour-washed to resemble closely those colours which were originally derived from the different sources of clay throughout Japan, shades of cream, 'bamboo' and pale terracotta being the most appropriate. If the location of the garden happens to be in a country where the clay tiles are imported, however simple they may be, this is a great advantage. However, where they are not available, a skilled potter can be commissioned to

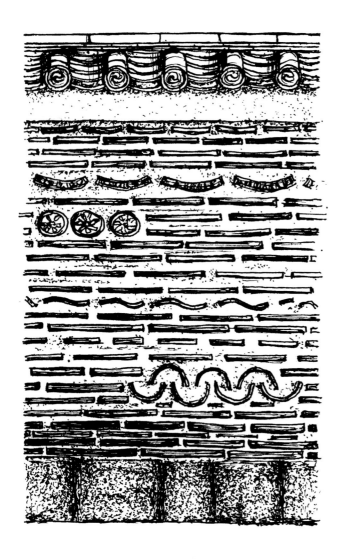

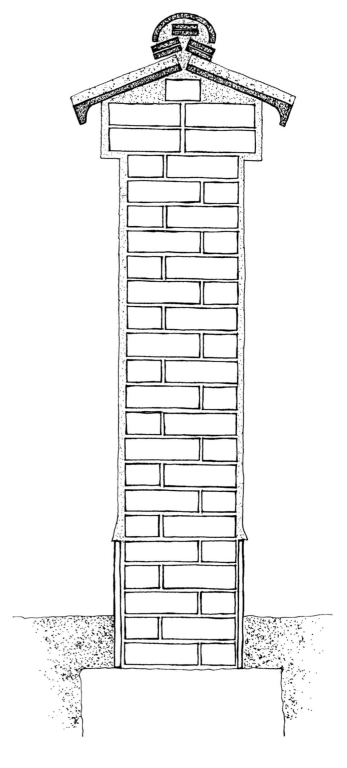

ABOVE: Neribei *(mud wall).*

RIGHT: *Wall profile.*

BELOW: *Tile-topped wall. Warwickshire, England.*

make them to order, with their installation undertaken by skilled and sensitive bricklayers.

Neribei *Walls*

Another, less familiar type of wall used as a boundary for temples or country estates is *neribei*. There are no short cuts in the building of this type of wall, the main structure of which is clay into which pieces of thin stone and curved tiles are embedded.

Fences

Bamboo Fences

The styles of fence in Japan are numerous and diverse, for the most part utilizing the plentiful supply of bamboo which thrives in the Far East. The construction of bamboo fences developed during the Momoyama period, with the growing popularity of the tea ceremony and its associated gardens.

KENNINJI-GAKI

One of the most familiar bamboo fences, often set on low stone walls, is made from uniformly cut and split bamboo, fastened vertically to horizontal crossbars, which, in turn, are supported by wooden posts. The number of horizontal supports used varies depending on the region of the country. Five tiers are mostly found in the west, whereas six tiers are popular in the east. Named after the Kenninji Temple in Kyoto, *kenninji-gaki* are frequently used as boundaries for Buddhist temple gardens. In common with many fence styles, *kenninji* fences are completed with uniformly tied black hemp, skilfully finished with distinctive knots.

GINKAKU-JI-GAKI

Ginkaku-ji fences, named after the Silver Temple (*Ginkaku-ji*) in Kyoto, have similar characteristics to the *kenninji* styles. *Ginkaku-ji* fences are typically set on a stone wall and are therefore lower and with fewer horizontal rails. More height may be provided by a clipped evergreen hedge, thus giving three disparate points of interest: the stone wall with random, rounded, greyish stones, the striking geometry of the honey-coloured bamboo and the green foliage of the living hedge.

SHIMIZU-GAKI

Of similar appearance at first glance are *shimizu-gaki*, *shimizu* fences, a name derived from the fine *shimizu-dake*, a bamboo which is used unsplit for the vertical element. In the West, where it is sometimes difficult to obtain the materials necessary to construct bamboo and other fences, this type can often be most readily mimicked by using screens or rolls of bamboo held together with strong wires. The whole screen can either

Ginkaku-ji fence.
Ginkaku-ji Temple, Kyoto.

Shimizu-gaki fence.
Ryoan-ji Temple, Kyoto.

be attached to existing Western-style fences or supported by a framework. Split bamboo crossbars, with distinctive, black hemp knots, complete this type of fence.

YOTSUME-GAKI

Another style of fence utilizes the individual canes which can easily be removed from rolls of bamboo; this is *yotsume-gaki*, four-eyed fence, which uses much less material than the *ken-ninji-*, *ginkaku-ji-* or *shimizu-gaki*, but can be labour intensive. To construct *yotsume-gaki*, horizontal poles are attached to the supporting posts and the bamboo is attached vertically to the poles, leaving evenly spaced gaps between. Sometimes the verticals are placed alternately to the front and the back, which gives added strength to the fence and is equally pleasing from both sides. Here too the finishing touch is the black hemp which is either 'woven' through and around the bamboo to hold it in place, or is knotted in the time-honoured way.

KINKAKU-JI-GAKI

Another distinctive fence is the *kinkaku-ji-gaki*, usually a low-lying fence which is used beside pathways or to divide the different parts of a garden. The open nature and low height of

Yotsume-gaki.
Kyoto.

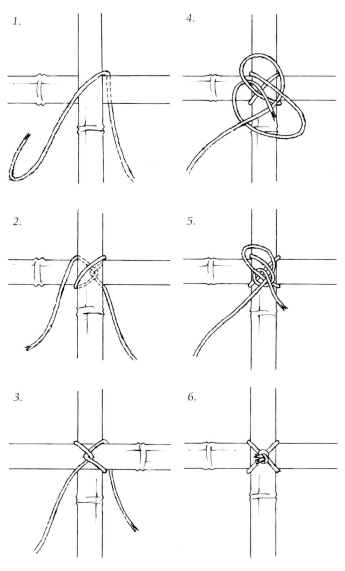

Knotting for yotsume-gaki.

Kinkaku-ji *fence.*
Kinkaku-ji Temple, Kyoto.

kinkaku-ji-gaki, also known as *shimoto-gaki* ('foot-level fence') is not designed to form a screen but mainly for decorative purposes. The construction is from large pieces of split bamboo, the most pronounced feature being the heavy-duty pieces which lie along the top, holding the fence in place and delaying the inevitable deterioration caused by weathering.

OTSU-GAKI

Where pliable, split bamboo is readily available it is used to make woven fences resembling wickerwork. The most favoured of such fences is the *otsu* technique. It is believed that the name originated from the fences lining the highway which passed through the city of Otsu in Edo times. To construct this

Otsu-gaki.
Saganō, Kyoto.

*Modern fence.
Kodai-ji Temple,
Kyoto.*

type of fence, horizontal bamboo poles are attached to supporting posts and the split bamboo woven between the poles. This technique requires flexible strips of bamboo cut recently and not dried out enough to become brittle.

MODERN BAMBOO FENCES

In modern gardens bamboo fences are still a vital element, adapting more traditional styles and using them as a backdrop to the garden composition rather than as an exterior boundary fence. Such fences are created for each garden where there may be a continuous run of vertical bamboo, as in *kenninji-gaki* or a simpler brushwood fence. However, the customary use of horizontal pieces is replaced by more random designs.

Bamboo Branch Fences

TAKEHO-GAKI AND *KATSURA-GAKI*

As well as the culms or canes of bamboo, the branches are used in constructing fences. Bamboo branch fences (*takeho-gaki*) may be made of strong or delicate branches, most commonly packed together vertically and held in place with the familiar horizontal split bamboo canes tied with black hemp. A notable exception to this technique is the *katsura-gaki*, named in recognition of the fence surrounding the Katsura Imperial Villa in Kyoto and the black bamboo which grows along the Katsura River, which was originally used in

its making. In this type of fence, horizontal rows of thick and thin bamboo branches are arranged alternately, with the vertical, supporting, split canes making an imposing feature, enhanced by thick knots of black hemp.

It is possible to create a reasonable facsimile *takeho-gaki* by using brushwood panels, set in place either with the brushwood running vertically and split bamboo tied on horizontally, or with the brushwood running horizontally and split bamboo forming the vertical element to nearly resemble the *katsura-gaki*.

All the materials used in creating these long runs of fencing are, traditionally, organic in origin and will deteriorate with time. In wet areas rotting will occur and in dryer ones cracking will adversely affect the pristine appearance. Some protection from the elements can be managed in several ways. Most commonly, materials other than the supporting posts are isolated from the soil by being set on stone walls, on a raised plinth or standing on a shallow row of natural stone. To prevent water from penetrating into the top of the cut bamboo, pieces of larger gauge bamboo are often tied along the top edge of the fence. Here the master knotter can really display his work with large, intricate creations, often sporting long, loose ends.

In some instances, a small roof is erected over the length of the fence, which may be finished with either thatch or cedar shingles. Supports for the roof need to be incorporated when building the fence, ensuring that the uprights are longer than the height of the fence and that they can be utilized as the basic framework for the roofing materials.

To prolong the useful life of cut bamboo it is advisable to apply two coats of clear, matt, yacht varnish, diluted with white spirit, allowing the first coat to dry fully before applying

ABOVE: Takeho-gaki.
Ginkaku-ji Temple, Kyoto.

ABOVE RIGHT: Katsura-gaki.
Katsura Rikyu, Kyoto.

RIGHT: *Reed and bamboo screen.
Private Garden, Kent, England.*

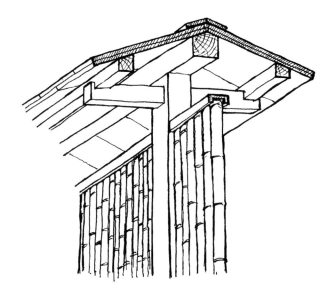

Fence roof construction.

the second. This procedure not only delays deterioration caused by rotting or splitting, it also protects the bamboo from fungal attack which causes discoloration and leads to deterioration. Traditionally, fences have been replaced regularly, sometimes annually, however, the expense and inconvenience of this are now more commonly delayed by using plastic substitutes where these are available.

Wing or Sleeve Fences

Wing or sleeve fences (*sode-gaki*) are small partition fences, frequently attached at right angles to the side of a building, giving the appearance of a kimono sleeve hanging from an outstretched arm. One of the most common places where *sode-gaki* are installed is next to a house entrance to provide screening. Although total screening can be achieved only with a solid object, many *sode-gaki* can be seen through, essentially acting as dividers.

Sode-gaki.
Shisen-do hermitage, Kyoto.

Sode-gaki have many other uses, whether to hide a utilitarian part of a garden or balcony, to form a backdrop for a water basin grouping or marking the transition from one part of a garden to another. The last is particularly effective when a Japanese-style garden is within a Western one.

Sleeve fences were conceived for use in tea gardens to separate areas or to provide privacy in limited spaces. Originally, they were made of brushwood or bamboo branches, arranged in varying styles, some intended to appear rustic, others more formal, but always constructed with precision and artistry. In common with boundary fences, the brushwood is held in place with split bamboo, sporting the typical black hemp knots.

Sode-gaki are also constructed from bamboo canes, particularly where full screening is required. Split bamboo is also used to make less dense latticework screens. A distinctive use of this technique is the *koetsu gaki*, a name derived from Koetsu Temple in Kyoto, where there is an easily recognized and atypically long specimen. Folklore describes this as having the appearance of 'a cow lying down in a field'.

Although there are publications giving instructions on how to construct sleeve fences, because of the difficulty and unpredictability in obtaining the requisite materials in the West, to buy units ready-made from an importer is a more promising approach. The choice of designs and sizes may be limited, but it is likely that suitable products can be found for almost any location.

ABOVE: Sode-gaki.
Private garden,
Dorset, England.

RIGHT: Koetsu gaki.
Private garden,
Kyoto.

THIS PAGE:
Shiorido *and brushwood
fence. Entrance to tea
garden, Sento Gosho, Kyoto.*

OPPOSITE PAGE:
*TOP LEFT: Agesudo.
Koetsu-ji, Kyoto.*

*TOP RIGHT: Thatched
gateway to tea garden.
Hakusasonsō, Kyoto.*

*BOTTOM: Entrance gateway.
Private garden, Nikko.*

Gateways

In Japanese gardens of any style, a gateway is the point of transition either from the street into the serenity of the garden or as punctuation within the garden. The simplest of gateways is largely symbolic, setting a change in mood; the grander and more elaborate ones indicate wealth and status.

Shiorido *and* Agesudo

The simplest and most economical gate is the *shiorido* (bent branch door), made by wrapping thin strips of bamboo sheath around a rectangular frame of round bamboo poles, with a resultant diamond-shaped pattern, supported on wooden posts. *Shiorido* typically mark the entrance to a tea garden from another part of a garden or act as dividers within a garden. Ready-made *shiorido* can usually be purchased from importers.

A taller version is suspended from a frame (*agesudo*) and can be raised with a bamboo pole to allow visitors to pass. *Agesudo* are a familiar feature of tea gardens.

Niwakido

Of greater stature are *niwakido*, which are gateways into the main garden. *Niwakido* may be made from rustic wood or bamboo and usually have a pitched roof meticulously crafted from bamboo, cedar shingles or thatch. *Shiorido* and *niwakido* are typically gateways bordered with bamboo fences, giving an informal and somewhat rustic feel. Where walls made of cedar planks or stone surround a garden, there are opportunities for more substantial gateways.

Modern Gateways

Within a domestic setting there are numerous variations in style and the use of materials for main gateways, which were traditionally for foot traffic but in more recent times have to accommodate the passage of cars and other vehicles. Gateposts may be of substantial cedarwood or stonework, often taking the weight of clay tile roofs. Pairs of gates will either swing on hinges, opening inwards, or slide across like screens.

Lanterns

Stone lanterns (*toro*) are a familiar sight in Japanese gardens and have been significant for many centuries. Originally, *toro* were used to light the front of Buddhist temples and were made of bronze, frequently with elaborate ornamentation. With the development of tea gardens in the Momoyama period (1568–1603) and the need to provide light for guests to negotiate the *roji* during the hours of darkness, temple lanterns were adopted as an integral part of the garden design. The placing of lanterns was always to provide light either near a gateway, at the turn of a path or near a bridge, a water basin or a well. The temple lanterns originally sited in tea gardens were somewhat large for the modest *roji* and, during subsequent periods, smaller models of different styles were designed and carved from natural stone.

Tachi-gata

Carved stone lanterns became popular in the Edo period, from 1603 onwards. Pedestal lanterns (*tachi-gata*) vary in height, some standing up to 3m (10ft), but small versions are more practicable for gardens. They are made in several sections, with a pedestal on which stands a shaft, usually round, which, in turn, supports the firebox and the roof. The pedestal

ABOVE: *Carved lantern beside water well. Gyokusen-en garden, Kanazawa.*

LEFT: *Bronze temple lantern, Nikko.*

and the firebox support sometimes have carvings of lotus petals. A carved lotus bud forming the topmost part of a lantern roof is a symbol frequently used in Buddhist artefacts.

Oribe-gata

One of the tea masters most instrumental in promoting *roji* was Furuta Oribe, who designed a style of stone lantern which bears his name. Unusually, the base of Oribe-type lanterns is buried in the ground. The shape of the shaft is square or rectangular, with a bulge at the top. The firebox is also rectangular, sometimes with a heavy roof resembling thatch.

ABOVE: Tachi-gata, Oribe-gata
and Oki-gata.

RIGHT: Bronze temple lantern.
Private garden, Dorset, England.

Yukimi-gata

A popular style of carved stone lantern is the *yukimi-gata*, the meaning of which may be interpreted as either having the appearance of a snow-covered hat or, simply, to facilitate the snow viewing. *Yukimi-gata* are typically low to the ground and supported on three or four legs rather than pedestals, with a large roof which may be hexagonal or octagonal. *Yukimi-gata* are most often sited near water, on either a rocky shore or an island, ideally where, following a fall of snow, passers-by can stop and admire the snow which has settled on the roof.

Oki-gata

Smaller still are *oki-gata*, movable lanterns, originally modelled on bronze temple lanterns, which either hung under eaves or were placed on a stone. The carved stone replicas are often sited near water, sometimes representing a lighthouse on a stone peninsula. In small gardens *oki-gata* are ideal for making an authentic statement when thoughtfully placed.

Oribe-gata. *School courtyard garden, Hampshire, England.*

may also be available, but so much is lost in quality that their value is limited – nothing can match the dignity of moss-covered, naturally-weathered stone.

Installing Stone Lanterns

The smaller lanterns such as *yukimi-gata*, *misaki-gata* or *oki-gata*, which are easily movable, may be placed in position without any fixing materials. However, the larger styles of stone lantern need more management and firm fixings. Implanted or *Oribe*-style lanterns are typically supplied in several sections. The base or pole needs to be set into the ground to the required depth. To ensure stability, it is advisable to set it in wet concrete, with a spirit level to ensure that it is vertical. When the concrete has set, the remaining parts of the lantern are placed on in order: first the central table, followed by the light compartment, the roof and the decorative lotus bud. The lantern should be sited so that the flat surface of the base and an opening in the light box are facing the viewer. A well-crafted *oribe-gata* may be sufficiently well balanced that the components will remain firm without any fixing materials. However, where pedestrians pass nearby it is sensible to use a transparent fixative between each part.

Similarly, a traditional, free-standing *toro*, such as the popular *kasuga-gata*, will be supplied in several sections. The broad base stone may stand on a level surface, but is safer when set into the ground. Prepare a hole for the base stone and tamp down, lining the bottom of the hole with firmed gravel or wet concrete. Place the base stone in the hole, ensuring that, when completed, the lighting window in the firebox will be at the front of the *toro*. The pole fits into a hole in the top of the base stone, followed by the supporting table and firebox, the roof and the decorative lotus bud. A transparent adhesive is again recommended.

The illumination of stone lanterns was originally provided by burning sticks or oils. In the modern world wax candles are more practicable, particularly those which are specifically made for outdoor use. Most stone lanterns are now supplied drilled for wiring and use electric light bulbs.

Lanterns for Japanese-Style Gardens in the West

Carved stone lanterns can be obtained in the West; these originate mostly in China and Korea, where there are plentiful supplies of granite and cheap labour. Although stonemasons still work in Japan, the prices of the finished articles are so high that only the privileged few can afford them. Consequently, Chinese and Korean imports are more common today. Replicas made of concrete, glazed clay or resins

Wooden Lanterns

With the availability of electricity it became possible to make lanterns out of more combustible materials, and wooden pedestal lanterns can now be seen in some traditional Japanese gardens. The use of wooden lanterns may be feasible in some locations within a Japanese-style garden in the West since they can be made by an adept carpenter, and the problems associated with handling the weight of granite are alleviated.

ABOVE: Cedarwood lantern.
Kenroku-en, Kanazawa.

RIGHT: Five-tiered 'Pagoda' lantern.
Heian Shrine garden, Kyoto.

Towers

Stone towers may also be used for lighting purposes, but are more likely to be decorative artefacts reminiscent of the five-storey pagodas of China and Japan, with their spiritual connotations. Towers have several tiers, always an odd number, of which five is adequate for most gardens. Stone towers are placed in similar positions to stone lanterns as well as on the tops of hills or complementing interesting trees.

4

Fusui in Japanese Garden Design

Geomantic principles in building and garden design have long been practised by the Chinese, partly according to beliefs that the universe is based on two opposing yet complementary principles of Yang and Yin, collectively named *Chi*. Yang (in Japanese, *yō*) is the positive component of *Chi*, considered to be male, light, sunny, creative, active, moving upwards, while Yin (Japanese: *in*) is the negative, is considered to be female, dark, wintery, wet, cold and moving downwards.

The Chinese sages who devised the principles of *feng-shui* – 'wind and water', Japanese *fusui* – believed that any man-made feature, be it a building, shrine, grave or garden could affect the flow of beneficial energy. They established the rules of placement that are central to the philosophy that man and nature must live in harmony with one another and that all life is infused with the invisible energy of *chi*, the belief being that this force circulates throughout the environment and is essential to our well-being, health and happiness. Simultaneously, the negative energy or *sha* needs to be eliminated from our environment to allow the free flow of *chi*. The Japanese adopted many of these principles, which they incorporated into the design of gardens and their orientation to associated buildings.

Approaches

Dwellings, especially in the West, usually have a front and a back entrance, with different aspects, auras and purposes. As *chi* energy flows quickly along straight lines, the Western tendency to have a straight path or driveway at the front of a building is not always ideal since the straightness will hurry the *chi* into the house, and, if the back door is aligned to the front, it will exit just as quickly. In many instances Japanese garden design paths do not go in straight lines; if the materials used are straight-sided, there may be a junction in the path and if the materials are less uniform in shape, especially when used as stepping stones, the paths will meander, slowing down the passage of positive energy.

Conversely, the ability of paths to encourage *chi* to flow quickly is desirable if the area at the end of the path is prone to cause the *chi* to stagnate. If there is a shady area or one tucked away from the rest of the garden where the *chi* cannot easily gain access, a straight path will help to bring this area into the garden as a whole. The skill is to ensure that paths take the *chi* where it is most wanted, at the speed it needs to travel.

Boundaries

Chi cannot be controlled until it reaches the garden boundary. It may derive from an area of *sha*, which is imbued with a negative energy after having passed through an unpleasant area. Boundaries are therefore considered as the first opportunity to gain control over or improve energies.

The height and the thickness of the boundary are the main aspects which will influence energies as they arrive. To encourage good *chi* it is recommended to use a boundary which is not too solid – for instance, an open-work fence, such as the bamboo 'four-eye' fence, so-called because of the four levels of openings created, or a stand of well-managed, live bamboo. Slightly more dense fences are made from brushwood, sometimes symbolizing a fence in the countryside. Hedges which are not too dense also allow the passage of positive energy.

To slow down *chi* higher or more solid boundaries are used. In Japan mud walls frequently enclose the buildings and gardens of temple complexes and the houses of the nobility and samurai. In areas where cedarwood, *Cryptomeria japonica*, grows naturally, it can be used to construct more solid fences.

Entrances

Entrances or gateways are integral to boundaries. Ideally, the garden entrance should be welcoming to *chi* and visitors alike. In Japan, until recently, natural materials were used to create entrances from the humble *shiorido*, most commonly used in tea gardens, through shingle and thatched gateways, to elegant cedarwood entrances which mark the transition to the inner world of the garden.

ABOVE: Cryptomeria japonica *boundary fence. Samurai house, Kakunodate.*

LEFT: *Bamboo hedge. Kyoto.*

In geomantic terms, when considering the style of the entrance, it is advisable to avoid solid doors in order to allow the *chi* to flow smoothly in and out. The main exception to this is when there is more than one entrance on one side of the garden, where it is desirable to restrict the flow of *chi* through one gateway, preventing it from becoming too strong. The more open the gateway, the more easily the *chi* can flow through it.

In common with boundaries, lower gates allow the energy to flow over the top, while gates of full height, especially those set into walls, fences or hedges, slow it down. In general, it is recommended that gates be left open. If a narrow or dark entrance needs more vitality, an open gate is more inviting than no gate at all, and emphasizes that the visitor is crossing a boundary. Conversely, an open south garden can acquire so much energy that it is not a relaxing place to be in. In this case opening a gate on to land which slopes away can let out some of the excess of energy and restore the balance of the garden.

Paths within the Garden

Within the garden the principles of *fusui* may be even more powerful. Paths are one of the most important features in many Japanese garden styles. They usually describe passages through various parts of the garden. The widespread use of stepping stones – *tobi-ishi* – in tea gardens could well be considered as an agent to control the passage of *chi*.

As with the periphery of gardens, *chi* passes more quickly along wider, straighter paths. When a path leads away from an open area it should be broad to make a smooth transition. However, it may narrow further on, as it ventures into more secret areas.

In the highly symbolic Zen *kare-sansui* dry gardens, stepping stones may hint at being a pathway. To cross *kare-sansui* gardens on foot is discouraged; however, there is an indication that *chi* energy is encouraged to pass through the expanses of raked gravel or sand. While such gardens tend to have very good *fusui*, *chi* is happiest in a garden with more life and greenery and, ideally, with real water.

Water

The use of water can lend enchantment to any garden and is a feature of modern gardening that we owe to the philosophy and experiments of ancient Chinese and Japanese gardeners. The natural streams which flowed through China were conceived as conveyors of wealth. Where possible, the Japanese divert streams through their gardens, creating artificial ponds which are endowed with *yō* qualities.

The wise men who were responsible for defining the powers of *feng-shui* became aware that the manner in which smoke was carried on the breeze and water ebbed and flowed along a river was indicative of how *chi* circulated throughout the environment. Geomancy says that rivers, streams, lakes, pools and even small ponds are potentially good conductors of *chi*. In parallel with the teachings on path configurations, it is considered that a river which meanders naturally across the countryside or a lake that forms a curved shoreline is better able to direct the flow of natural energies than a watercourse which runs in a straight line or has sharp bends.

It is also believed that the energy quotient of a garden pond is improved by stocking it with fish or terrapins. Gold and silver fish are specially recommended as they symbolize valuable coins and wealth and are especially prized by

Gold and silver koi.
Isui-en garden, Nara.

koi enthusiasts. Terrapins, which can survive long periods in water, are believed to bring long life and stability.

Plants

Plants are also endowed with *in* and *yō* qualities, and their choice and placing also affect the energies within a garden. Seasonal plants having *yō* characteristics are of particular value. An early herald of spring is the Japanese plum or apricot *Prunus mume*, locally called *ume*, its *yō* character heavily symbolic of vitality and rebirth. The *chi* of a garden can be enhanced by placing a *ume* near water or a gateway. Historically, the Chinese cast the petals of plum flowers into rivers in the hope of attracting wealth and good fortune.

As spring unfolds, so do the flowers of azaleas, signalling that the harsh bleakness of winter is past. As well as symbolizing delicacy and having the positive aspect of *in*, it is believed that azaleas aid the flow of *chi* with their funnel-shaped flowers and light-green whorls of leaves. In late spring the flowers of wisteria come into their own. Often festooning specially made bamboo pergolas, sometimes beside a pond, wisteria also has particular qualities and, in the opinion of many *fusui* experts, no garden is complete unless it contains at least one correctly sited wisteria.

Other plants familiar to Westerners are camellias. It is believed that the camellia has the most attractive leaves of any flowering shrub and its handsome, glossy, evergreen foliage is a good conductor of *chi*, especially when it is planted against a wall or pruned into a hedge. Highly prized in Japan, where it is known as 'living jade', *Camellia japonica* cultivars flower in late spring, and the scented *Camellia sasanqua* flowers in autumn. Autumn is a time when Japan is clothed in vibrant scarlets, oranges and yellows. The most abundant providers of these hues are the maples – *momiji* or *kaede*. Significant in terms of *fusui* is the paper-bark maple, *Acer griseum*. Discovered centuries ago in central China, with chestnut-coloured bark and delicate, young, green leaves which will turn scarlet in autumn, it is considered one of the most decorative of foliage trees providing a firm defence against bad *sha*. In common with other maples, the flowers open in May and hang in bunches, later developing into winged seeds which float on the breeze, indicative of successful flight.

Another of autumn's glories is *Gingko biloba*, which is believed to attract friendship to the owner of the land on which it stands. *Fusui* warns never to prune the gingko, as shortened shoots will die back just as a friendship can wither. However, practical considerations often overwhelm this belief and gingkos are regularly pruned and shaped.

One of the most versatile groups of plants to enhance the *fusui* of a garden is that commonly referred to as bamboo. In addition to the belief that the flexibility of bamboo is akin

Azaleas beside path.
Jonangu-ji, Kyoto.

ABOVE: Acer griseum, Ginkgo biloba *and* Acer palmatum
'Osakazuki' awaiting planting. Private garden, Dorset, England.

*ABOVE RIGHT: Pruned bamboo over a garden wall.
Private garden, Fushimi, Kyoto.*

to being a true gentleman, it was believed by the ancient
Chinese to be a symbol of virtue, possessing strong powers,
and has long been used in garden plantings as protection
against evil spirits and inclement weather. In Japan, the practice of removing lower leaves of bamboo, with a cluster
remaining at the growing tip, is believed to ward off bad *sha*,
and can often be glimpsed above a garden wall.

In the Far East, bamboos of varying heights, girths and
colours, flourish and are widely planted. In moderate climates the choice is more limited since many of the larger
varieties require the higher temperatures and humidity to
foster the rapid growth rates. Of those readily available to
Westerners, and a complement to any garden is *Phyllostachys
nigra*, the black-stemmed bamboo which provides positive
fusui in any garden throughout the year.

The System of Five Elements

In addition to the positive or negative forces brought to a
garden by its design and the inclusion of beneficial features
and plantings, there is the ancient Taoist system of Five Elements, which represents a sequence of changes. When in a
smooth, flowing, cycle these elements form a creative cycle:
wood fuels fire; fire creates earth; earth creates metal; metal
can flow like water; and water feeds wood. When the harmonious cycle is not maintained and the elements become
out of sequence, a cycle of destruction results.

In *fusui* this cycle is acknowledged, but not so strictly
implemented as in Chinese architecture and gardens. It is
interesting, however, that the Japanese naming of days of
the week includes these five elements: *nichi-yobi* – Sun-day;
getsu-yobi – Moon-day; *ka-yobi* – Fire-day (Tuesday); *sui-yobi*
– Water-day (Wednesday); *moku-yobi* – Tree-day (Thursday);
kin-yobi – Gold-day (Friday); and *do-yobi* – Earth-day
(Saturday), thus recognizing their importance within the
geomantic whole.

5

Plants and Planting

Introduction

The cultivation, choice, positioning and maintenance of plants in Japan has a unique place in garden history and design. No rolling lawns and herbaceous borders here, no patchwork of rockery plants and shrubs, very little in the way of free-flowing tree shapes. Plants are selected partly for their symbolism and partly for their shape, foliage and flowering habit. Quality is more important than quantity, each specimen being selected for a particular place and planted with great attention to its orientation and importance within the whole composition.

Plants native to Japan are numerous and include a wide spectrum of herbaceous, shrub and tree species, many of which are also available in the West and can often be identified by the specific epithet *japonica*, from Japan. The selection of plants satisfactory for gardens has evolved through the centuries and depends to a large extent on what will survive in a particular climatic zone. As the land form of Japan is an archipelago, stretching through several latitudes, with long sea borders and prominent, dramatic mountain ranges, there are many micro-climates. In the northern island of Hokkaido winters are long and cold with short days. The main island of Honshu varies from cold and wet in the north, through hot, humid summers and cold dry winters on the plateaux, with increasing temperatures to the south. The island chain which reaches further southwards from Kyushu towards Okinawa is even drier and less hospitable.

Ground-Covering Plants

Plants used for ground cover are among those most susceptible to temperature and moisture changes since they have shallow root structures and tend to cover sizeable, exposed surfaces.

Mosses grow well in areas where there is plentiful rain and some shade and have long been used in temperate areas of Japan as a luxuriant ground cover, sometimes allowed to colonize and sometimes deliberately planted. The garden of the Saiho-ji Temple near Kyoto has so successfully been colonized by numerous different mosses that it has been re-named *Kokedera*, 'The Moss Garden'.

Planting moss.
Private garden, Kyoto.

Moss has been used for ground cover for many centuries, enhancing tea gardens and strolling gardens associated with palaces and temples and is often the carpeting material surrounding stepping stones. Moss is also planted in some *kare-sansui* gardens to anchor the standing stones to the surrounding sands or gravels, and to give the appearance of islands. Most commonly used is haircap moss, *Polytrichum commune*. In domestic gardens mosses are also cherished and purposely introduced. Due to its wide usage, moss is commercially cultivated in Japan and sold in slabs. The slabs are broken into smaller sections about 60mm (2.5in) square, placed at intervals on the prepared soil and tamped down with a flat tool. In areas where there are hot summers it is imperative to water daily or be prepared to replant in the autumn. Where moss is not available an excellent substitute is *Soleirolia soleirolii* syn. *Helxine soleirolii*, which, in common with moss, is considered by some to be a nuisance. Its positive characteristics are that it is evergreen, will survive dryer conditions than moss, is readily available and will not only successfully spread and cover large areas in a few months, but will also fill in crevices and soften hard edges. A disadvantage is that it will go black following a hard frost, but does regenerate in time. As with mosses, *S. soleirolii* is divided into pieces and planted into the prepared soil.

Soleirolia soleirolii, 'mossy' mound.
Private garden, Dorset, England.

Dividing Ophiopogon japonicus
'Tamaryu'. Temple garden, Kyoto.

BELOW: Sasa veitchii.
Plant nursery, Kyoto.

Low-growing bamboos provide useful ground cover, especially under trees and shrubs where they prevent weed growth and soil drying The species most favoured for ground hugging are *Pleioblastus pygmaeus, P. pumulis* and *Sasaella ramosa*, which are kept short and robust by regular cutting back with shears or a strimmer or by mowing with a high-set mower blade. Cultivated bamboos are most likely to be supplied in pots, from which they can be costly to attain a quick covering, unless the plants are easily divided. Bamboos are eminently useful for stabilizing slopes since their rhizomes bind together the topsoil. Even though they will grow in a wide spectrum of conditions, it is particularly important to ensure regular watering, especially in the first years of planting and on slopes which drain rapidly.

Sasa veitchii, which grows to a height of approximately 1m (3ft) and is particularly shade tolerant, is frequently used in woodland or in bamboo groves as a ground cover. Once established, it is vigorous and spreads rapidly. The maturing leaf margins of *S. veitchii* become dry and creamy in colour, making them particularly attractive in heavily shaded places. Also useful in shady places is *Pachysandra terminalis*, a hardy, low-growing sub-shrub, native to woodland, which makes a good ground cover and spreads well.

In recent times, prostrate conifers such as *Juniperus chinensis procumbens* 'Nana' and *J. horizontalis* have become popular as ground cover due to their dense and ground hugging growth habits. Usually pot grown, planting should be at a spacing appropriate to size when mature. Overcrowding in early years is counterproductive.

Creating green swards from mowable grasses is a suitable option in temperate zones. However, where there are

Another hardy, evergreen and good-natured plant, frequently used for ground-covering and crevice-filling is *Ophiopogon japonicus* (*tamaryu* – 'Dragon's whiskers'): a grasslike monocotyledon which multiplies well, is low growing and thrives in shade as well as being heat-tolerant and suitable for use where the climate is adverse for growing mosses. *Tamaryu* is also grown commercially in Japan, typically in shallow wooden boxes. Before being planted it is manually divided into smaller clumps which are planted at uniform spacings of approximately 100mm (4in) and watered in. In due course, the clumps will spread and will grow together, forming a dark green, uniform mat.

ABOVE: Juniperus horizontalis *and
snow-viewing lantern. Koko-en garden, Himeji.*

Polystichum *fern and stone grouping.
Private garden, Kyoto.*

unusually cold winters or hot summers there will be periods when any grass will deteriorate. If there is a prolonged period of lying snow or heavy frost, grasses will lose condition and turn brown. Temperate grasses will also become brown in drought conditions and tropical grasses such as *Zoysia* will discolour in colder winter temperatures.

Accent Plants

Accent plants often accompany features such as rock placings, water basin groupings and stone lanterns, creating a pleasing transition between the upright, hard materials and the horizontal plane. Ferns such as *Polystichum polyblepharum* and *P. rigens*, both of which are evergreen and hardy, may often be seen at the base of rock placings where they appear to have grown naturally. Ferns prefer moist, shady places and will not thrive in full sun or drought conditions.

Hosta species, many of which originated in Japan, can be planted where conditions are similar to those enjoyed by ferns. The disadvantage of hostas is that, being herbaceous, they die back in early autumn. Unless carefully managed hostas also fall prey to slugs and snails which feed on and destroy the soft, leafy tissue. *Gentiana makinoi*, an erect, herbaceous perennial with leafy stems bearing pairs of lance-shaped, bluish-green leaves and blue flowers in the late summer, can also be planted at the base of or between rocks.

Gentiana sino-ornata and *G. ternifolia*, which originate in China, are also appropriate for use in Japanese-style gardens. The first is a rosette-forming, semi-evergreen perennial with many prostrate shoots bearing finely pointed, dark green leaves; stalkless, blue and purple striped, trumpet-shaped flowers appear in the autumn. *G. ternifolia* is a vigorous, trailing, semi-evergreen perennial, with loose rosettes of greyish leaves, in the autumn bearing striped blue flowers on the prostrate stems. To grow well, gentians need humus-rich, moist but well-drained soil that is neutral or slightly acid. In areas with warm, dry summers shade is necessary.

Moisture-loving plants are excellent accent plants adjacent to water basin groupings. *Ligularia tussilaginea* syn. *Farfugium japonicum*, an evergreen plant with long, straight stems, bearing large, glossy, kidney-shaped leaves also prefers fertile, moist but well-drained soil and partial shade. In contrast, the upright, thinly stemmed rush *Equisetum hiemale japonicum* makes a striking companion to a water basin and thrives in soil dampened by water overflowing the basin's rim.

Another upright plant often used as an accent is *Miscanthus sinensis* and its cultivars, herbaceous perennials with upright, reed-like, arching stems, with pale green or bluish leaves. The terminal arching panicles have a silky appearance and are borne in late summer and autumn. It is planted so that the autumn sun highlights the shimmering inflorescences; it is fully hardy and tolerant of most conditions, preferring moderately fertile, moist but well-drained soil in

Gentiana ternifolia.
Daitoku-ji, *Kyoto.*

Miscanthus sinensis *in the evening sun.*
Ryoan-ji Temple, Kyoto.

Nandina domestica. *School courtyard garden, Hampshire, England.*

Mahonia japonica, *overhanging water basin outside a coffee shop, Kyoto.*

full sun. Stems should be cut to the ground by early spring. *M. yakushimensis* is a denser, clump-forming species growing to 60cm (24in) with long, light green leaves with pink midribs turning yellow in autumn.

Sometimes an accent shrub or small tree is planted behind a water-basin feature or lantern. Most customarily sited in this way is *Nandina domestica*, or 'Heavenly bamboo' (*nanten*), an evergreen shrub with upright stems and pinnate foliage which is flushed red in the spring and purplish red in the autumn. In the summer conspicuous panicles of small, white flowers appear above the foliage, turning to waxy red berries in autumn and winter. A close relative of *Nandina domestica* is *Mahonia japonica*, an erect evergreen shrub with serrated, glossy leaves and racemes of fragrant, pale yellow flowers in winter, followed by dark blue berries. Mahonia is tolerant of full sun where the soil is rich in humus and does not dry out. However, it does prefer complete or partial shade.

Shrubs

The planting of shrubs extends beyond accent plantings to those which are used in planting schemes, bearing in mind that in Japanese gardens most plantings are in moderation. Many of the species and cultivars listed below are suitable for a wide range of climatic zones and micro-climates.

Abelia chinensis: semi-evergreen, native to hillsides and open woodlands, cultivated for the profusion of flowers in autumn; it is well suited for sunny sites, responds well to hard pruning and is sometimes used for informal hedging.

Ardisia japonica: a compact shrub with erect, clustered stems and glossy dark green leaves; in summer bearing corymbs of star-shaped, white to pink flowers, followed by bright red berries; prefers shady, moist, well-drained conditions and is ideal for underplanting.

Pruning Buxus microphylla japonica. *Private garden, Kyoto.*

BELOW: Camellia japonica. *Private garden, Hampshire, England.*

Aucuba japonica: vigorous bushy, rounded, evergreen shrub with glossy, mid-green, spotted leaves; grows wild in shady mountain areas, valued for its hardiness, shade and pollution tolerance; female plants bear bright red fruits in the autumn; if *A. japonica* becomes leggy or overgrown it will regenerate quickly following heavy pruning.

Azalea: see *Rhododendron*.

Berberis thunbergii: a bushy, rounded, deciduous shrub with sharp spines, which grows on hills and mountains all over Japan; the young foliage is pale green above and bluish-green beneath; in mid-spring racemes of yellow flowers are produced along the branches, followed by red fruits; fully hardy, it will grow in well-drained soil in full sun or partial shade; responds well to hard pruning and makes a useful hedge.

Buxus microphylla japonica (Japanese box): grown mainly for its foliage; a slow-growing evergreen shrub with mid- to deep-green leaves; grows in any fertile, well-drained soil, preferably in partial shade; well known in Western temperate climates; used in topiary and for edging parterre gardens, thanks to its dense growth habit and acceptance of hard pruning; sometimes grown as a hedge, especially on top of walls, or maintained in ball shapes to represent rocks.

Callicarpa japonica: a deciduous shrub with arching stems carrying sharply elliptical, toothed leaves which turn pinkish in autumn; inconspicuous flowers followed by bright purple, bead-like berries in late summer and autumn. It is called *Murasaki-shikibu* by the Japanese, named after the lady who, in the Heian period, wrote the famous *Tale of Genji* which tells of court life in the eleventh century, including descriptions relating to the enjoyment of gardens.

Camellia japonica: a strong growing, shrub or small tree; the glossy, dark green leaves have finely toothed margins; flowering from early to late spring in colours ranging from white to dark red; *C. japonica* and its cultivars are used as specimen plants as well as for screening and hedging; they should be positioned in partial or dappled shade and sheltered from cold, drying winds and early morning sun.

Camellia sasanqua: bears scented flowers in the autumn and is more tolerant of full sun provided that the roots are kept cool; all camellias prune well, and to highlight individual flowers, branches may be thinned out, reducing the number of blooms produced.

Chaenomeles japonica: sometimes referred to as 'flowering quince' or simply 'japonica', a well-recognized, sparsely branched shrub treasured for its early flowers which are cup-shaped, single or double, borne individually or in clusters; the autumn fruits may be cooked and eaten; often trained against a wall or useful as ground cover or low hedging; *C. japonica* is tolerant of heavy pruning and shade, but flowers and fruits better in full sun.

Enkianthus campanulatus: a spreading deciduous shrub, occurring naturally in scrub and woodland, cultivated for racemes of bell-like flowers, borne from spring to early summer, and for leaves which turn various shades of red in the autumn; prefers humus-rich, acid to neutral soil and will grow in full sun or partial shade.

Euonymus alatus: a dense, bushy, deciduous shrub with toothed, dark green leaves, which turn brilliant dark red in autumn; grows naturally in thickets and woodland and valued for the autumn foliage and winged fruits which split open to reveal additional colourful seed coverings; may be hard pruned to form a rounded profile.

Euonymus japonicus: dense, evergreen shrub with leathery, dark green, toothed foliage, useful for hedging.

Eurya emarginata: another dense, evergreen shrub or small tree with leathery, dark green leaves, tinged red in winter; although half hardy, tolerates salt wind in warmer climatic zones.

Eurya japonica: slow growing evergreen shrub, which prefers partial or complete shade and will tolerate dry soil; sometimes used a hedging around tea gardens.

Clipped Euonymus alatus.
Isui-en, Nara.

Fatsia japonica syn. *Aralia japonica*: distinctive evergreen shrub with large, leathery, palmate leaves produced at branch tips, with umbels of creamy white flowers borne in the autumn, followed by clusters of small, black fruits; will tolerate sun, but prefers partial or full shade.

Hydrangea macrophylla: rounded, deciduous shrub with broad, coarse-toothed, dark green leaves, bearing flat corymbs of pink or blue flowers in late summer to autumn on previous year's growth; to prune young plants in early spring cut off previous season's flower heads to a pair of buds beneath each flower; for mature plants cut back about one-third of the oldest shoots to the base to promote replacement growth. Used as a hedge beside pathways.

Ilex crenata (commonly known as box-leaved holly or Japanese holly): an evergreen shrub or small tree with small, scalloped, glossy, dark leaves; sometimes used for hedging, more familiarly as specimens trained and pruned into 'cloud' forms.

Kerria japonica: deciduous, suckering shrub with arching green shoots found in thickets and woodlands of China and Japan; the sharply toothed, pale green leaves appear in mid to late spring, accompanied by single or double golden yellow flowers; usually grown as a specimen in full sun or partial shade.

Ligustrum japonicum: an upright, dense, evergreen shrub with glossy, mid-green leaves, white flowers are produced from midsummer to early autumn, followed by black fruits; fully hardy, it will grow in any well-drained soil in full sun or partial shade; makes a good hedge which will need regular trimming.

Osmanthus fragrans: a vigorous, upright shrub or small tree with leathery, finely toothed, glossy, very dark green leaves, bearing fragrant, tubular, white flowers in autumn and sometimes in spring and summer; useful as a specimen plant or hedge, especially against a sheltering fence or wall.

Osmanthus heterophyllus: a more rounded species, producing sweetly scented flowers in late summer and autumn; needs fertile soil in sun or partial shade, with shelter from cold, drying winds; prune in spring.

Photinia glabra: dense, evergreen shrub with large, oblong leaves which are bright purple-red when young; in summer bears panicles of small white flowers, followed by red fruits, eventually turning black; can be used as a specimen or for hedging; prune late winter or early spring when dormant.

Pieris japonica: compact, rounded, evergreen shrub with glossy, mid-green leaves, bright red when young, fading to white; in spring bearing panicles of white, tinged pink, flowers; there are numerous cultivars of *P. japonica* with varying growth habits and flower colours; most usually planted as a specimen, in humus-rich, moist but well-drained acid soil, in full sun or light shade.

Pittosporum tobira: rounded, dense, large shrub or small tree with erect stems and obovate, leathery leaves deep green

Pieris japonica. *Private garden, Hampshire, England.*

above and paler beneath, with recurved margins; in late spring and early summer bears large clusters of bell-shaped, sweetly scented, creamy white flowers; semi-hardy; needs protection from cold, drying winds.

Rhododendron syn. *Azalea*: the cultivars widely planted in Japanese gardens are evergreen with unscented flowers in a wide range of colours, borne in early spring and are particularly effective in mass plantings; Kyushu and Kurume hybrids are very hardy, low-growing cultivars with small, shiny leaves; Satsuki hybrids were originally developed for bonsai working, they are less hardy and bear large, funnel-shaped flowers in summer which are white, pink, red or purple, sometimes multicoloured; all varieties are used for low hedging or to represent rocks whether singly or in clusters and are heavily pruned to maintain tight growth and uniform shapes.

Spiraea japonica: clump-forming, deciduous shrub with erect shoots and dark green leaves, grey-green beneath; in mid and late summer bearing pink or white flowers in terminal corymbs; tolerant of hard pruning, useful as a ground cover for small areas.

Spiraea nipponica: a larger deciduous shrub with arching branches; leaves and flowers similar to those of *S. japonica*; used as a specimen or in clumps.

Wisteria floribunda: deciduous climber found in Japan in moist woodland and on stream banks, often seen twining through large bamboos; cultivated for fragrant flowers which are borne in pendant racemes in late spring; colours vary from white to pink, mauve and shades of purple; usually grown over specially constructed bamboo pergolas, at a height where the masses of flowers come into view as one approaches; so highly regarded is wisteria that its local name is shared with that of the revered mountain Fuji.

Wisteria floribunda *on bamboo pergola. Jonangu-ji Temple, Kyoto.*

BELOW: *Hedge-pruning techniques.*

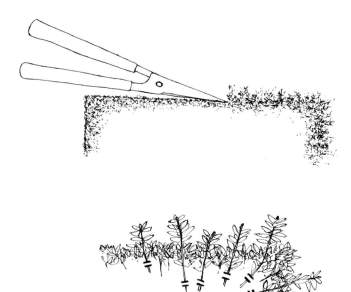

Hedges

Hedges grown in and around Japanese gardens rarely resemble those familiar in the West, although their functions may be similar. Perimeter screening hedges are frequently planted on top of stone retaining walls. Walls vary in height up to about 1m (3ft), the combined height of wall and hedge invariably amounting to about 2m.

To provide all-year-round screening, shrubby evergreens, which are amenable to regular pruning, are most frequently chosen. Wall top hedges are meticulously pruned, typically into squared-off, boxy shapes. Pruning involves not only regularly cutting back the new foliage to retain the required shape and size, but, equally importantly, removing any dead material and spindly growth and thinning out healthy growth annually to allow for light penetration and air circulation and to encourage new growth within the hedge. These procedures ensure that vigorous growth is maintained throughout the entire planting and the pattern of straggly woody growth in the centre with heavy foliage on the margins is avoided.

Favourite plants for such hedges are *Ardisia japonica, Buxus microphylla japonica, Camellia japonica, Euonymus japonicus, Ilex crenata, Ligustrum japonicum* and *Rhododendron* cultivars. In some cases the hedging material, such as *Juniperus chinensis* and its cultivars, and *Chamacyparis obtusa*, is carefully trimmed into rolling shapes, sometimes resembling ocean waves or even passing clouds.

The planting of hedges around dwellings is a valuable contribution to the greening of the urban landscape. In some areas of Japan, families who plant hedges instead of erecting fences receive financial subsidies.

Low-growing hedges are a prominent feature of shrine and temple gardens, usually beside a path, either on the approach to the temple entrance or within the confines of the garden. In these situations hedges are maintained to a height and width of about 60–70cm (24–28in), with regular trimming and pruning to preserve strong and healthy growth throughout the planting. The plants most used in these situations are *Rhododendron* (azalea) cultivars or *Buxus microphylla japonica*. In addition, hedges can be used to form backdrops for garden compositions and to create a striking

ABOVE: *Trimmed* Camellia japonica *and* Rhododendron *hedges. Private garden, Kyoto.*

ABOVE RIGHT: *Shaped* Juniperus chinensis *hedge. Private garden, Kyoto.*

RIGHT: *Clipped* Rhododendron *hedge. Daitoku-ji* *Temple complex, Kyoto.*

*Clipped double hedge,
Ryogen-in, Kyoto.*

Trained Camellia sasanqua *on bamboo
framework. Higashi Geisha district, Kanazawa.*

contrast when forming part or all of the framework for a *kare-sansui* garden.

Short runs of hedging are erected where a barrier is required. Within a garden such a barrier might direct visitors from one route on a pathway to another, or used to screen an unsightly area. At the entrance to buildings, hedging screens occasionally disguise doorways and focus attention on negotiating the screen. Where there is limited space, a bamboo support is constructed to which heavily pruned screening plants are attached.

Selecting Shrubs and Hedging Plants

Having formulated a plan for the proposed garden, the selection of the appropriate shrubs and hedging plants is a priority. It is important to test the soil and establish its acidity

or alkalinity; Japanese soils are mostly derived from the breaking down of volcanic rocks and tend to be acidic. Therefore the plants which naturally colonize the landscape and grow well in cultivation are those which prefer acidic soils, with an acidity below pH 7 (local knowledge and soil-testing are the best ways of ascertaining pH). When it is desired to create a Japanese-style garden in areas of alkaline soils, those plants which are lime-tolerant need to be chosen, which limits the choice and excludes many which are most closely associated with Japanese gardens.

When choosing plants, look for those which are in good heart. Evergreens should have shiny leaves and supple, new growth; conifers should have plentiful foliage which is not brittle to the touch nor turning brown. When in leaf, deciduous plants should also have healthy foliage and obvious signs of potential new growth; during the dormant period it is possible to discover whether a deciduous plant is healthy by scraping back the bark – if green and sticky wood is revealed, the plant is healthy, if brown, that part of the plant at least is dead and indicates that further dying back will ensue.

When choosing container-grown plants, where it is possible, remove the plant and the root ball from the pot. If the roots are tightly bound together and brownish, the plant is pot-bound and will probably not grow well when planted in the garden. Roots should be whitish and fairly loose, with the potting medium still crumbly.

Theoretically, pot-grown plants can be planted at any time, but this is inadvisable unless regular irrigation can be supplied during the summer. The optimal time for planting is autumn when the soil is still warm but cooling; temperatures are dropping, and leaf fall is imminent. Aided by wetter weather, autumn planting gives recently planted shrubs a chance to settle into their new environment ready to restart active growth in the spring.

It may be preferable to acquire plants which are either bare-root or root-balled (ball and burlap). Such plants have been grown in open ground from which they have been lifted for planting. Bare-root or root-balled plants are less expensive to buy than those which have been container-grown and are ideal when the budget is a consideration or there are large areas to be planted. Lifting, and therefore planting, can be done only in the dormant (winter) period which, in the Northern Hemisphere, is from November to early March.

Planting Shrubs

Whether containerized or not, the planting principles for all shrubs are very similar. A planting hole is prepared; depending on the quality of the soil, additional organic material is added, ensuring that it is mixed with the native soil around the perimeter of the hole, with a substantial layer of it in the bottom of the hole. If the soil has a high clay content the perimeter of the hole should be broken up, avoiding the formation of a sink which does not drain.

Plants should be watered before planting, ensuring that the compost and roots are well wetted. When possible, it is advisable to tease some of the young roots away from the root ball so that they begin to seek water and nutrients from their new home and do not stay restricted to the container compost or original root ball. Bare-rooted plants are ideally suited to having their roots spread out within the planting hole. All gaps are filled with the organic material, whether it is a proprietary compost or home-made compost, and tamped down to fill all air pockets. Water in all new plantings and continue to irrigate during dry periods. When supports are required, they should be introduced at the time of planting, taking care that the roots are not damaged by driving stakes into the vulnerable root zone.

Deciduous Trees

Flowering Cherries

There are several groups of plants which are quintessential hallmarks of Japanese gardens, among the most treasured and familiar are those referred to as 'flowering cherries' (*sakura*), the welcome heralds of spring, bringing hope for the future and the assurance of rebirth.

There is a large diversity of flowering cherries (*Prunus*) which occur naturally in woodland and woodland margins, as well as in harsher, rocky places. Those which are the most admired for reliable, prolific flowering tend to be deciduous, with flowers opening before foliage appears. Flower colours range from white, through pink to dark red. Single flowers are distinctive, with five clearly visible petals, each with a 'notch' at the tip. Stylized artistic interpretations of the *sakura* flower have, for centuries, appeared on Japanese china, as delicate embroidery on silk kimonos and as a decal on roofing tiles. *Sakura*-shaped sweets are popular in modern-day Japan. The petal shape is not so apparent in semi-double and double flowering varieties such as the upright *P. amanogawa* and *P.* 'Kanzan', but the heavy flower heads are more showy and spectacular. Some *Prunus* cultivars have interesting bark, such as *P. serrula* with shiny, peeling, dark red bark, which glows in sunlight.

Those *Prunus* varieties which are popular for planting in gardens are fully hardy and grow in any moist but well-drained, moderately fertile soil, the deciduous varieties preferring full sun. The first *Prunus* to flower is *P. mume*, Japanese apricot or Japanese plum, called *ume* by the Japanese, with bowl-shaped, fragrant white to dark pink flowers, produced singly or in pairs in February or early March, followed by green-yellow fruits in summer which are used in pickles and cordials. *P. mume* is long-lived and greatly respected, so much so that in the courtyard at the main entrance to the former Imperial Palace in Kyoto it is one of

Stylized 'Sakura' motif, clay roofing tile.
Chishaku-in garden, Kyoto.

only two plants given honoured places. To prune it – in winter after flower buds are formed – reduce the branches with buds by one-third and cut back spurs without buds. *P. mume* 'Pendula' is a weeping form with pink flowers.

The flowering cherries which open in late April are those which create the greatest excitement among the Japanese and which prompt the cherry blossom festivals (*sakura matsuri*)

and blossom-viewing parties (*o-hana mi*), where the nation celebrates with picnics and all-night partying. It is commonplace to see plantings along river and canal banks where visitors can stroll and admire the fragile blossoms.

Prunus jamasakura syn. *P. serrulata* var. *spontanea*: the mountain cherry, believed to have originated on Mount Yoshino, near the ancient capital of Nara, is a spreading, deciduous tree with oblong leaves which are bronze when young, turning red and yellow in autumn.

Prunus yedoensis (Yoshino or Tokyo cherry): a spreading tree, with arching branches and dark green leaves, with a profusion of racemes of bowl-shaped pink flowers, fading to nearly white; 'Shidare-yoshino' has weeping branches which cascade to the ground.

P. 'Shidare sakura' is another weeping variety bearing white or pink flowers on pendulous branches and is long-lived and highly revered in Japan; the branches of large specimens are festooned over fan-shaped trellis supports so that their beauty can be fully appreciated, some ancient specimens are so highly treasured that they are registered as national monuments and bear an identifying plaque.

In his *Secret Teachings in the Art of Japanese Gardens*, David Slawson refers to an entry in a fifteenth-century manuscript compiled by the priest Zōen, entitled *Illustrations for Designing Mountain, Water and Hillside Field Landscapes*, which states that;

> While the Japanese cherry may be found most anywhere, on mountain peaks, mountainsides, or in the deep mountains, you must chiefly bear in mind villages when you plant it. The cherry is also fascinating when planted in the juncture between the deep mountains and the verdant hills. For its 'home site', bear in mind the south. You may also plant one or two cherries

ABOVE: Prunus mume.
Enryaku-ji Temple, Kyoto.

RIGHT: Sakura matsuri.
Kakunodate.

in the shade of trees that are associated with high or remote mountains, so that one feels there is a village nestled deep in those mountains. Really, the cherry, possessing the special qualities that it does as a tree, may be planted in any location whatsoever without difficulty, so long as you plant one specimen in the cherry's home environment. A person who has not received the transmission, even when given two or three trees to work with, will plant them so indiscriminately that not one will be in the cherry's home site, and thus will incur the blame of those who have received the transmissions. In all such matters you must act with a similar discernment.

This is a clear endorsement that, when selecting plantings and deciding on their positioning in Japanese-style gardens, great attention should be given to imitating their natural habitat.

Maples

For centuries maples have infiltrated the gardens of the Japanese. During the Edo period (1603–1868) interest in their selection and breeding heightened. As more species of maple were found and cultivars developed, many were given romantically descriptive names.

Maples are treasured for their delicate spring foliage, often brightly coloured, their summer foliage balanced and trembling on shapely branches, but especially for their autumn colouring. Although not usually thought of as flowering, many Japanese maples have attractive and colourful, small flower clusters, hanging like Christmas tree ornaments below the fresh spring foliage, followed by winged fruit in late summer.

Some maples – *momiji* or *kaede* – have interesting bark, such as *Acer palmatum* 'Sango kaku' (coral bark maple) which has bright, coral-coloured, smooth bark, and *A. griseum* (paper bark maple) with a peeling, dark-red or rich chestnut bark, complementing the distinctive green leaves which turn to orange and red in the autumn. The large variations in growth form, leaf and bark colour and branching habit provide choices for several uses in gardens small or large. *A. palmatum* and its natural cousins grow in a diversity of environments on the islands of Honshu, Shikoku and Kyushu. Many thrive in the West, particularly on soils which are slightly acidic.

Green varieties and cultivars with large leaves will usually take full sun, but it is advisable to provide some afternoon shade to prevent scorching. For the same reason, it is vital that, when planted in containers, the compost is never allowed to dry out. Similarly, to protect roots from frost in winter is wise.

Acer japonicum: full-moon maple, produces leaves which are rounded, lobed and toothed; a popular cultivar is *A. japonicum* 'Aureum', syn. *A. shirasawanum* 'Aureum' which has a compact growth habit and bears bright yellow leaves which turn red in autumn.

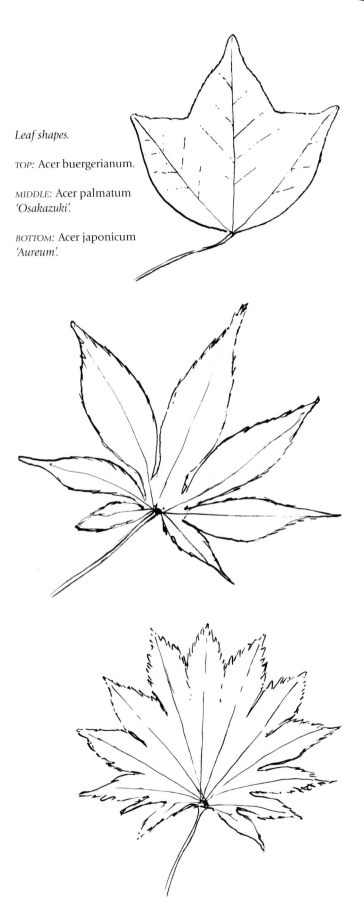

Leaf shapes.

TOP: Acer buergerianum.

MIDDLE: Acer palmatum 'Osakazuki'.

BOTTOM: Acer japonicum 'Aureum'.

Acer palmatum.
Daitoku-ji *Temple complex, Kyoto.*

Newly planted Acer palmatum,
Women's University campus, Kyoto.

Once established, maples grow quite rapidly, and in a Japanese-style garden pruning and shaping are undertaken regularly to maintain an open and delicate shape, allowing the light to illuminate the layered branches. The dappled sunlight encourages moss and other ground-cover plants to grow.

As winter approaches and the maples' foliage changes to vibrant reds and oranges, the leaves which fall may be briefly left to be enjoyed, or a few individually selected and floated on the surface of water. Maples are often planted to represent a natural woodland, with branches overhanging paths or walkways, or they may be used as specimens, elegantly enhancing a stone water basin or lantern. In order to achieve the overhanging, asymmetrical growth of maples, their planting is stage-managed. Trees are planted at an angle so that their heads lean towards a path or bridge, or overhang a stone artefact, giving the appearance of growing naturally on a hillside. To sustain this contrived growth habit, strong two- or three-legged tree supports are strategically placed, with a

crosspiece to which the trunk is tied with a natural sisal string. When the tree has become established in the desired shape, the supports can be removed.

Other Deciduous Trees

Cercidiphyllum japonicum (Katsura): a deciduous woodland, multi-trunked, pyramidal tree with heart-shaped, pale green leaves, turning scarlet or pink in autumn, at the same time releasing a sweet, vanilla-like scent; hardy in temperate zones and prefers rich, neutral to acid soil in sun or partial shade.

Cornus florida: flowering dogwood; although not native to Japan it is often planted as a specimen; first introduced as a gift from the USA in exchange for the blossoming cherries which surround the reflecting pool in Washington, DC.

C. florida is a conical, deciduous tree, with broad, oval mid-green foliage, which is slightly curled and turns bright red in autumn; the showy bracts of white, pink or red, which have a notched or pinched tip, festoon the spreading branches in spring; most prolific in areas with hot, humid summers; frost-hardy, preferring fertile, humus-rich, neutral to acid soils in sun or partial shade.

Cornus kousa: a broadly conical, deciduous tree with flaking bark and dark green leaves with wavy margins, turning deep red in the autumn; in summer, showy notched bracts unfold, surrounding inconspicuous flowers; 'Satomi' has dark pink bracts and dark red-purple autumn foliage, making a striking specimen plant.

Diospyros kaki (Japanese persimmon, *kaki*): a deciduous, small tree found in forests in tropical, subtropical and warm-temperate regions; prized for its attractive, open growth habit, the simple leaves, which are often glossy, turning yellow to orange-red and purple in the autumn, and particularly for its fleshy, orange-coloured, edible fruits which hang on the bare, dark brown branches into late autumn (these are often represented in woodblock prints and other media); can be grown in deep, fertile, well-drained, loamy soil in full sun, sheltered from cold, drying winds and late frosts; prune during the dormant period.

Ginkgo biloba (Maidenhair tree; *icho*): an upright tree, columnar when young, wider spreading when mature, with furrowed, dull grey bark; characteristic fan-shaped, two-lobed, leathery, pale green leaves which change to golden yellow in the autumn; a prehistoric tree, believed to be the residence of spirits and often planted adjacent to Shinto

ABOVE LEFT: Cercidiphyllum
japonicum *branch.*
Private garden,
Hampshire, England.

ABOVE: Diospyros
kaki *bearing fruit.*
Private garden, Kyoto.

LEFT: Cornus florida rubra.
Kyoto Flower Centre, Kyoto.

shrines; in domestic gardens the glowing autumn foliage complements the reds and oranges of maples and stands out against dark green pines; fully hardy and tolerant of urban pollution, will grow in any fertile, well-drained soil in full sun; prune in dormant season.

Magnolia hypoleuca (Japanese big-leaf magnolia; *ho-no-ki*): a vigorous, conical, deciduous tree with large, mid-green leaves up to 40cm (16in) long; followed by fragrant, creamy-white flowers with prominent red stamens in late spring and early summer; will grow in temperate climates, in moist, well-drained, humus-rich soil, preferably acid to neutral, in sun or partial shade, with shelter from strong winter winds.

Magnolia kobus: a broadly conical, deciduous tree, native to hillsides, where the white flowers are borne in March/April, before leaf burst, giving the illusion of a snowy covering; the flower buds are pointed, shaped like a fist, prompting the Japanese name *kobushi* (a fist); branches carrying flowers or seeds are used in *ikebana* flower arrangements.

Paulownia tomentosa: decidous woodland tree, producing strong, quick-growing shoots and large, heart-shaped, hairy, mid-green leaves; fragrant, purplish flowers are borne in upright racemes before leaf burst; grows and flowers best in climates with long, hot summers, in fertile, well-drained soil in full sun; in frost-prone areas, shelter from cold, drying winds; when cut, the wood of *P. tomentosa* does not warp with changes in humidity and has traditionally been used in making furniture and clogs (*geta*); prune in the dormant season; stylized representations of the leaves and flowers are often seen in architectural details.

Leaf shape.
Ginkgo biloba.

Sophora japonica (Japanese pagoda tree): vigorous deciduous tree found in tropical and temperate regions in dry valleys and woodland, as well as on rocky hillsides; in late summer and early autumn, mature trees bear small, fragrant, pea-like white flowers, followed by hanging fruit pods; prefers

Stylized Paulownia tomentosa *flower motif. Momoyama Castle, Kyoto.*

moderately fertile, well-drained soil in full sun; in frost-prone areas needs winter protection; prune in dormant season.

Stewartia pseudocamellia: broadly columnar, deciduous tree native to woodlands, grown for their peeling, pink to red-brown bark and dark green leaves which turn yellow to orange and red in autumn; rose-like, cup-shaped white flowers are borne in midsummer; grow in moist but well-drained, moderately fertile, humus-rich, neutral to acid soil in full sun or dappled shade; prune in dormant season.

Evergreen Trees

Several species of evergreen tree are used in Japanese gardens. Those most familiar are the conifers, often referred to as 'pines', which have an important place in ancient and

Hand-pruning Pinus thunbergii *branch. Private garden, Kyoto.*

modern Japanese culture. The significance of pines in Japanese mythology and legend is described in Chapter 1.

'Pines'

The concept of training and pruning pines into unusual shapes was introduced by the early Chinese settlers, who brought with them ink drawings and paintings, as well as ceramics which depicted deep mountains and valleys, and islands in the sea on which grew windswept pine trees. It is this weathered appearance, implying longevity and strength in harsh habitats, which is frequently replicated by using long established training and pruning techniques.

'WINDSWEPT' PINES

Pines readily lend themselves to being shaped, either as garden or bonsai specimens. To train a young tree into a 'windswept' shape for ultimate garden use, lengths of bamboo are tied to branches, bending them in the desired direction. Black hemp, similar to that used to tie bamboo fences, is used to tie the bamboo poles to the pliable branches. When the branches have lignified, the bamboo poles are removed. If it is required that a branch bends downwards to overhang water, for instance, a stone weight is hung from its tip.

In order to maintain the desired shape, every cluster of needles on the tree is thinned out by hand, usually at the end of the growing season, leaving only upwardly pointing needles and denuding the underside of branches. New growth (or 'candles') are also thinned out; by controlling how much of each candle remains, the shape and general direction of the branches can be determined, and all the energy goes into making foliage and not cones for reproduction. Some large pines will take several professional gardeners each two or three days to hand prune, at the same time removing any dead and diseased growth and any branches which are detrimental to the desired shape. Diligent pruning also ventilates the tree and permits sunlight to reach every bough, thus minimizing pests and diseases and encouraging healthy growth.

Japanese pruning techniques tend to accentuate, at an early stage, the lines of the trunk and the branching structure of the tree. The Japanese black pine, *Pinus thunbergii*, and the much prized Japanese red pine, *P. densiflora*, respectively representing the seashore and the mountains, lend themselves to the manipulative techniques which result in a windswept appearance. Both these species bear long needles grouped in peglike pairs. When the pairs of needles fall naturally in the autumn, they sometimes settle on the branches of plants below, an image which is often reproduced by artists. Specimens of *P. thunbergii* are often trained by the use of bamboo

Extended Pinus thunbergii *branch.*
Bono Ike Temple, Kyoto.

or other supporting materials to produce one predominant, horizontal branch which is sometimes encouraged to reach several metres in length. Such specimens are usually placed beside an entrance where they span the gateway.

'CLOUD' PRUNING

In contrast to the naturalistic, windswept style, a shaping/pruning technique often employed on pines and other evergreens is 'cloud' pruning where layered pads of growth are developed over many years in spirals around the trunk, suggesting that there is a heavenly place which can be reached by climbing the stairway of clouds. This technique is effectively applied to the Japanese white pine *P. pentaphylla* syn. *P. parviflora*, which, in its natural form, is a conical or columnar tree with purplish brown bark. The dark green leaves are borne in groups of five, giving the Japanese name of *goyomatsu* (*go* is five). This is particularly useful for shady places.

Taxus cuspidata (Japanese yew): has short, spiny-tipped, dark green leaves, turning reddish in winter; amenable to cloud pruning; *T. cuspidata* is hardier then its better known, near relative, *T. baccata*.

In regions with high rainfall or summer humidity, *Podocarpus macrophyllus* (*kusamaki*) is a popular garden choice for a cloud-pruned specimen, an evergreen tree, with reddish brown bark and erect or spreading, yellowish green shoots and mid-green, narrow, lance-shaped, leathery leaves; needs protection from cold winter winds; *P. macrophyllus* 'Maki', with smaller leaves is a much prized variety.

OTHER PRUNING AND TRAINING TECHNIQUES

A 'pine' familiar to Westerners is *Cryptomeria japonica* (Japanese cedar, *sugi*); one of the largest native trees in Japan; with long, straight woody growth, it is ideal for use in building and furniture making. In domestic gardens *sugi* are pruned in a unique manner. Early in its growth, the trunk is cut

Shearing cloud-pruned Podocarpus macrophyllus.
Private garden, Kyoto.

Pruning Cryptomeria japonica.
Private garden, Kyoto.

slightly above the ground, thus encouraging multiple stems to form, at the top of which the leafy growth becomes a pompom shape. It is especially useful where there is limited space, such as beside a boundary wall where the top growth is revealed above.

With the limited land available for houses and gardens, the sight of methodically pruned or shaped 'pine' trees rising above boundary walls is typical of Japan. Familiar forms include the creating of layers of branches in whorls around the trunk, which, in turn, is cleaned of all unwanted new growth. The undersides of the branches are stripped of greenery and the remaining clusters of needles on the top-side are thinned out in the customary way.

Conifers such as *Chamaecyparis pisifera* 'Filifera' which have drooping, flattened sprays of foliage and do not produce terminal candles are differently managed. Most of the foliage is removed along the length of the branches, leaving pendant tufts at the branch tips. The thinning out is achieved manually and undertaken at the end of the spring/summer growing season and again in late autumn.

Pruned Chaemaecyparis.
Private garden, Kyoto.

WINTER PROTECTION

In areas of heavy snowfall, specimens with spreading branches which, in some cases, have been tended for centuries, are protected from being broken under the weight of snow. The branches are supported by hemp ropes radiating from a vertical, supporting pole. The resulting conical shape is, in itself, a beautiful sight, the ropes being meticulously and symmetrically placed (*yukitsuri*). The procedure is carried out annually in domestic gardens, plantings in the street, as well as in large public gardens. The most notable example is at the Kenroku-en Garden in Kanazawa in the Japanese Alps, where the pine trees give the garden structure and form in winter and are most picturesque when blanketed with snow, silhouetted against an ink-black sky.

CHOOSING 'PINES'

The pines mentioned above are mostly hardy in temperate zones. Care needs to be taken with *Podocarpus* spp. which are somewhat tender. Most species native to Japan are readily available in the West, although they are usually grown in traditional Western styles. They will thrive in most soils, with the exception of heavy, wet clay. Imported 'cloud'-pruned trees are available, but, due to their great age and the cost of the labour which has been invested over many years in their shaping and care, they tend to be somewhat expensive. However, in the right setting they are breathtaking. With knowledge and time, some of the other shapes which make a Japanese-style garden more authentic can also be achieved.

Other Evergreen Trees

Cinnamomum camphora (camphor tree): an erect to spreading tree with narrow, boldly veined, glossy dark green leaves, greenish-red when young; small, bowl-shaped, flowers are borne in spring and summer, followed by black berries; prefers moist, but well-drained soil in sun or partial shade; to thin out the thick foliage, remove crossing and unwanted

Cloud-pruned Ilex crenata.
Private garden, Dorset, England.

Protecting evergreens for the winter: yukitsuri.
Private garden, near Fukui.

branches in winter or early spring; a tree which requires warm temperatures, the smell of camphor exuding on sunny, humid days; widely planted in shrine gardens and public parks; due to its longevity many specimens are considered sacred.

Cleyera japonica: grown for its attractive, thick shiny foliage and pale yellow to creamy white flowers borne in early summer; grows only in warmer climates and often planted in shrine gardens; *C. japonica* is the sacred tree of Shinto, its branches are offered at altars and on ceremonial occasions; believed to be the first tree that grew out of the chaos of creation; grows in acid, moderately fertile soil, in sun or partial shade, sheltered from cold, drying winds; prune after flowering to maintain required shape.

Cycas revoluta (Japanese sago palm): found mainly on dry, stony slopes and in semi-desert and dry, open woodland; robust, stemmed cycad, erect at first but gradually suckering, branching and reclining when mature; first introduced into Japanese gardens in the Momoyama period, often used to imply a rocky hillside. A well-known grouping known as the 'Cycas Hillock' in the garden of the Katsura Imperial Villa, Kyoto, can be viewed from a roofed bench, where guests wait to be summoned for the tea ceremony at the Shokintei pavilion; hardy only in warmer climatic zones; to protect from winter chill the ingenious Japanese encase the tender trunks and foliage in rice straw.

Eriobotrya japonica (loquat): vigorous, spreading tree with stout shoots and bold, sharp-pointed, strongly veined, dark green leaves, with brown, felt-like undersides, up to 30cm (12in) long; bearing large panicles of fragrant white flowers from autumn to winter, followed in early summer by

ABOVE: Cinnamomum camphora *following autumn pruning. Private garden, Kyoto.*

LEFT: Cycas revoluta. *Tiger Glen Garden, Nishi-Hongan-ji Temple, Kyoto.*

spherical, edible, orange-yellow fruit; because of its over-winter flowering, the optimum fruiting is achieved in areas with mild winters; its siting in gardens needs to be chosen with care, as the spreading branches and dense evergreen foliage can create a dark, damp area beneath in which few plants will survive; prune during the dormant period.

Quercus myrsinifolia: rounded, evergreen tree with smooth, dark grey bark and lance-shaped, tapered, glossy, dark green leaves, bronze-red when young; tolerates pollution and sea air and also tolerates clay and lime-containing soils; can be used as a windbreak, hedge or a specimen; prune in dormant season.

Ternstroemia japonica syn. *T. gymnathera* (*mokkoku*): evergreen tree occurring in woodland in mainly tropical regions; bearing leathery, glossy, very dark green leaves, turning bronze in cold weather; white flowers are produced in late spring and early summer, following by greenish-yellow berries, ripening to red; can be grown as a specimen or for hedging; prefers rich acid soil and partial or complete shade; prune in early summer by removing the longest central stem from each new growth; not frost-hardy.

Selecting and Planting Trees

Having established an outline plan for the garden, it is important to select trees with care. Typically, in Japanese-style gardens, each tree is treated as a specimen and selected for its size, shape and place. Choices may be purely aesthetic or take into consideration symbolism, mythology and/or *fusui*.

Before making a final choice, as with all plantings, it is advisable to establish the soil type and pH, as well as the microclimate of the proposed position of each plant. Although it is possible to make improvements in soil structure and small adjustments to the pH, to ensure the most successful growth and longevity it is advisable to choose those trees which have the greatest chance of surviving the ambient conditions. This is particularly important, obviously, when investing considerable sums of money in mature trees.

Mature trees are planted in Japan when gardens are created so that the finished scene appears to have been there for many years. Traditionally, nursery-grown, mature trees are readily available, enabling the established effect to be

Mature cloud-pruned Podocarpus macrophyllus. *Tree nursery, Kyoto.*

achieved. Some nurseries have for sale trees which are up to 200 years old.

Choosing Trees

As with shrubs, look for trees which are healthy: evergreens with shiny leaves and supple new growth, and conifers with plentiful foliage. Also look at the trunks and bark and select specimens with intact bark and good trunk shapes. If there has been any grafting, ensure that the graft unions are strong and have knitted together successfully. Reject any plants showing signs of stress or disease.

Root-wrapped Cryptomeria japonica.
Tree nursery, Kyoto.

Planting Trees

In theory, container-grown trees can be planted at any time of year. However, the same principles apply as with all other plants, it being advisable not to plant during hot, dry periods unless regular irrigation can be supplied. In Japan, root-balled trees are mechanically lifted, with a large volume of soil remaining intact; hessian is wrapped around them to prevent loss of soil and moisture and the whole is neatly bound with sisal string. When planted, the hessian and string remain, both being natural products which will eventually break down. Whether container-grown or root-balled, the preferred planting time is during the dormant period. The planting hole is prepared to a depth and width approximately 30 per cent greater than the diameter of the root ball.

If the soil has a high sand or clay content, well-rotted organic material or a proprietary tree planting compost should be mixed with the native soil. A layer of this material is placed in the bottom of the planting hole to such a depth that, when the tree is planted, the surface of the root ball will be just below the soil surface; this will minimize drying out.

The tree is placed in the hole at the required angle. To ensure the natural, wind-blown appearance some species are planted at an angle of 30–45 degrees to the perpendicular. At this stage, plant supports can be hammered into the ground, taking care not to damage the root ball. Finally, fill in the spaces with the organic material or planting compost, treading it down to exclude air pockets, and water well. In some instances it may be advisable to provide a submerged, perforated pipe into which a hose can be inserted to ensure that water will reach the lower parts of the root system. Tie the tree to the supports with sisal string and protect the trunk from chafing with a hessian binding.

Tree-planting.
Private garden, Kyoto.

Bamboo

Traditionally, bamboo is known as one of the 'Three Friends of Winter', together with 'pines' and *Prunus mume* (*see* above). There are over a thousand species of bamboo, many of which originated in China. Low-growing forms, such as *Pleioblastus pygmaeus* and its cultivars and *Sasa veitchii*, make good ground cover, especially in shady conditions. By contrast, the giant *Dendrocalamus* spp., which are robust with rapidly spreading rhizomes, produce culms up to 30m (98ft) in height and 30cm (12in) in diameter. The largest cultivars are not frost-hardy and require high summer temperatures and humidity to achieve rapid growth rates.

Some live bamboos do grow well in Western climates, their unique growth habits enhancing diverse situations. The taller growing forms are useful for accent plantings as well as for living screens. In addition to being evergreen, the diversity of growth habits, stem colours and leaf sizes make bamboos desirable in domestic gardens. The sound of bamboo leaves rustling in the breeze is reminiscent of water flowing, stimulating cool and calm thoughts. Bamboos can be enjoyed in a variety of situations and, in addition to their garden use, they are amenable to limitations of a courtyard or terrace and are tolerant of urban pollution.

In Japan, there are many traditions associated with bamboo; for instance, only certain species are used for making the equipment so central to the tea ceremony. In some parts there is a 'bamboo-splitting festival', which originated in the eighth century, a ceremony which is blessed by priests, opening the way for young men to split the fresh canes. Split bamboo is used in many ways, most notably in making fences and screens.

Since bamboo is an intrinsic part of the Asiatic landscape it has for centuries been illustrated on ink drawings and scroll paintings. At one time there were specialist bamboo artists in Japan creating elegant paintings for the Imperial Court. Live bamboo was first brought to Europe in the middle of the nineteenth century, when silk importers took hitherto unknown plants back from the Far East as gifts for their clients or for their own enjoyment. As little was known about bamboo, those which arrived in the West were the ones most able to survive the long journey by ship, most notably the hardy *Phyllostachys* spp. Interest was aroused in Europe and by the early twentieth century over 200 species were available, more tender species surviving in the warm climate of southern France. In the USA, particularly in the warm climates of the South and the West Coast, there are now several significant collections.

Below are listed some of the bamboos most successfully grown outside East Asia.

Chusquea culeou: a graceful, erect bamboo, with thick, solid culms, forming clumps of glossy, yellow-green to olive-green canes, having a striped appearance when young; distinctive tessellated, mid-green leaves almost encircle the waxy nodes; grows to 5m (16ft) and hardy to –15°C.

Fargesia murieliae syn. *Arundinaria murieliae*: clump-forming bamboo, with light green arching culms maturing to deeper green and yellow; bright green leaves; ideal for hedging, reaching 3–4m (10–13ft) and not too invasive; hardy to –25°C.

Fargesia murieliae 'Simba': clump-forming cultivar, more upright than *F. murieliae*, with yellow-green culms and light green leaves; grows to 2m (6½ft) and hardy to –25°C.

Fargesia nitida syn. *Arundinaria nitida*: slow-growing bamboo, forming a dense clump of erect, dark purple-green culms, with narrow, dark green leaves; will remain compact without constant attention; grows to 2m (6½ft) and hardy to –25°C.

Phyllostachys aurea: clump-forming, upright bamboo with grooved canes, mid-green when young, maturing to golden when grown in full sun; bearing narrow, yellowish to golden green leaves; grows to 4–5m (13–16ft) and hardy to –15°C; excellent specimen plant.

Phyllostachys aureosulcata 'Aureocaulis': vigorous, clump-forming, upright cultivar, with rich yellow culms; good for

Phyllostachys aureosulcata *'Aureocaulis'.*
Nursery, Hampshire, England.

screening or as a specimen plant; grows to 6m (20ft) and hardy to −20°C.

Phyllostachys bambusoides 'Castillonis': upright, vigorous cultivar, with thick, golden yellow culms and green internodal grooves giving a striped appearance; very striking specimen plant; height up to 8m (26ft), hardy to −20°C.

Phyllostachys bissettii: very strong species with erect, grey-green culms and dark green leaves; good for hedging or screening; very hardy, remaining attractive throughout the winter; height up to 5m (16ft), hardy to −20°C.

Phyllostachys nigra: one of the first ornamental bamboos to be introduced to the West; clump-forming with arching, slender culms green when young, turning to lustrous black in second or third year, especially in full sun; produces abundant dark-green leaves; in temperate climates grows to 5m (16ft) and hardy to −25°C.

Phyllostachys violascens: clump-forming, then spreading bamboo, with swollen green canes, becoming striped with shades of brown and violet-purple; fairly invasive; height to 8m (26ft), hardy to −25°C.

Pleioblastus auricomis syn. *P. viridistriatus*, syn. *Arundinaria aurocoma*: upright bamboo with hollow, purple-green culms and long, linear leaves which are bright yellow, striped green, particularly in full sun; height to 1.5m (5ft), hardy to −15°C.

Pleioblastus pygmaeus syn. *Arundinaria pygmaea*: upright, woody bamboo, with slender culms and small, neat leaves; grows to 25–30cm (10–12in) and hardy to −15°C; can be mown to form a dense ground cover.

Pseudosasa japonica: upright, thicket-forming, robust bamboo, with olive green canes when young, maturing to pale beige and medium to large dark green leaves; good for hedging and screening; grows to 3m (10ft) and hardy to −20°C.

Sasa veitchii syn. *S. albomarginata*: spreading, low-growing bamboo, with large, creamy marginated leaves; ideal for ground cover in shade; height up to 1m (3ft), hardy to −25°C.

Sasaella ramosa syn. *Sasa ramosa*, syn. *Arundinaria vagans*: very vigorous, low-growing bamboo with slender culms and medium-sized leaves, having a narrow, withered margin in winter; good ground cover for large areas; height up to 1m (3ft), hardy to −30°C.

Shibataea kumasasa: low-growing, clump-forming bamboo, with dense, dark green foliage; new shoots appear in early spring; likes a warm, damp site and is ideal for ground covering; height up to 80cm (32in), hardy to −21°C.

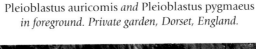

Pleioblastus auricomis *and* Pleioblastus pygmaeus *in foreground. Private garden, Dorset, England.*

*Stylized sixteen-petal chrysanthemum flower motif.
Clay roof tile, Imperial Palace, Kyoto.*

BELOW: *Exhibition of large-flowered chrysanthemums.
Nishi-Hongan-ji Temple, Kyoto.*

Selecting and Planting Bamboos

Although containerized bamboo plants are available from nurseries and garden centres throughout the year, the optimum time for planting is late spring and early summer, when the plant has ample reserves to produce new culm growth, followed by rhizome formation in the summer. If autumnal planting is the only option, it is important to ensure that new plantings are well watered and protected from drying winds and frosts. It is better to choose plants which are reasonably young and actively producing plentiful rhizomes and new culms.

Bamboos prefer a soil which is moderately fertile, moist but well-drained, and do not thrive in heavy clay or predominantly sandy soils. Although they need abundant supplies of water, they do not like permanently saturated soils such as those with a high water table or which are naturally boggy.

When planting, prepare a hole 50 per cent deeper and wider than the diameter of the container or root ball. Place some of the chosen planting compost in the bottom of the hole so that, when planted, the top of the root ball is slightly below the surface of the surrounding ground. Fill in the gaps, cover the top of the root ball with compost and tamp it in; water well. Mulching with organic material will help to reduce water loss.

Chrysanthemums

Although not strictly an integral part of garden design, the growing of chrysanthemums in Japan is a skill which has long been practised and perfected. Their importance in Japanese culture was recognized by the Imperial Family, who adopted a single sixteen-petalled flower as their emblem. The status of Emperor is referred to as 'sitting on the Chrysanthemum Throne'. The Imperial Order of the Chrysanthemum is the highest honour in the land.

Cultivating Chrysanthemums

Large-Flowered Varieties

EXHIBITION CHRYSANTHEMUMS

Typically, decorative chrysanthemums (*kiku*) are pot-grown, with meticulous attention to details of disbudding, tying, feeding and watering. During November, on the front porches of many houses, displays of three perfect, long-stemmed

*ABOVE: Chrysanthemum cascade.
Street scene, Kyoto.*

*RIGHT: Chrysanthemum five-tiered pagoda and model deer.
Nara Municipal Offices, Nara.*

specimens, a majority of which are reflex varieties, are proudly shown to all visitors. These heavy-headed specimens need to be reliably supported and special pots are made with three holes just below the rim to which bamboo canes are tied. A circular wire frame, which can be moved up the canes as the plant grows, supports the blooms.

Exhibitions of chrysanthemums grown in this way are a regular sight in public places, such as outside town halls or in the approaches to temples and shrines. The group of cultivars used for growing such specimens have long been known as 'Large Exhibition' and until recently were internationally known as 'Japanese chrysanthemums'.

Smaller-Flowered Varieties

CASCADES

Smaller flowered varieties are used to create cascades, dolls and bonsai specimens. Cascades are developed using small, single-flowered varieties to produce a solid mass of flowers which resemble a tumbling waterfall or traditional bride's bouquet. The young plants are potted at a 45 degree angle, with supporting stakes. As they become larger, bamboo or wire frames are substituted, through which new shoots are woven and pinched back to ensure uniform flowering. Skilled growers can achieve cascades up to 1.5m (5ft) long and 60cm (24in) wide. These masterpieces are also displayed for public

enjoyment, sometimes within the garden, or amongst a collection of potted plants in a street frontage.

DOLLS AND OTHER MODELS

Small flowered chrysanthemums are also used to create chysanthemum dolls, which may portray human or animal forms – a technique which began in the early nineteenth century and has been revived in the late twentieth. Young plants are inserted into bamboo and straw frames and planted into sphagnum moss. The skilful training and pinching of the emerging shoots encourages short stems and prolific flowering which covers the framework.

BONSAI

Chrysanthemums are also widely grown for bonsai work, a creative art requiring patience and dexterity but little space. Chrysanthemums are particularly suited to this art form,

Chrysanthemum 'bonsai'.
Nara Municipal Offices, Nara.

larger pots and, finally, into the bonsai container, at the same time the roots are pruned if necessary to limit any further growth, and the soft wires are removed.

When cultivating pot-grown chrysanthemums for any of these uses, the local climatic conditions need to be considered. In zones with hot, humid summers, air cooling devices will be necessary, and in those with cool winters, protection and heating will need to be provided.

Hardy Plant Bonsai (*bon*: a tray, *sai*: plant cultivation)

Similarly to the cultivation of chrysanthemums, the art of bonsai is a horticultural technique practised in Japan over many centuries. The heavily manipulated, miniature specimens or groupings of trees and shrubs that are universally recognized and admired are not used in a garden setting. Bonsai plants command prominent places in which to be displayed. Most usually they are set out on slatted, wooden benches, elevated so that they can be more easily admired and worked. To prevent damage by the elements, plants need to be protected from wind and full sun and are often provided with overhead screening materials.

Bonsai collections are highly prized and respected by their owners who generously want to share their achievements with others. Displays are often glimpsed in limited spaces beside or in front of dwellings. Some valuable collections are protected by security fencing and guard dogs. Owners of significant collections are keen to explain the importance of particular specimens, pointing out those which have been admired by the Emperor and other notables.

In common with early Japanese garden designs, the concepts and techniques of bonsai originated in China over 2,000 years ago, where the ancient Chinese wanted to bring representations of their much loved hillside landscapes into their own spaces. Many shapes and treatments of trees, especially 'pines', have been developed to create facsimiles of native trees clinging to barren hillsides, nestling in windswept crevices or defying the elements on isolated islands. Originally the Chinese collected stunted plants from hillsides and displayed them in pots or trays. Subsequently, training and pruning techniques were developed to restrict and manipulate the growth habits of trees and shrubs, thus creating miniature scenes.

growing more quickly than woody plants, as well as being pliable and bearing many flowers on short stems. With time and patience, a finished specimen may be ready within twelve to fifteen months of taking cuttings in the early autumn, ready for exhibition the following year. After rooting, cuttings are planted in potting compost in small pots. In early spring when new growth begins, the shoot tip and any large leaves are removed. The growing branches are encouraged into the desired shapes with soft wire and developing shoot tips continue to be removed. As the plants increase in size and form thick stems resembling tree trunks, they are transferred into

Bonsai collector and guest. Private garden, Kyoto.

BELOW: Euonymus alatus *cascade. Bonsai exhibition, Kyoto.*

Apart from chrysanthemums, the plants commonly used for bonsai are hardy and prefer to be outside so that air can circulate and natural, if filtered, sunlight can reach the foliage. On occasion, a particular specimen may be taken into the dwelling for the enjoyment of family or guests. In Japanese houses special alcoves or *tokonoma* are built in which bonsai

specimens or *ikebana* flower arrangements are displayed, traditionally accompanied by a hanging scroll with a complementary naturalistic scene and appropriate calligraphy.

In Japan, bonsai exhibitions are major undertakings, with classes for various techniques and species of plant. Stalls carrying pots, composts, tools, accessories and plants are in abundance and advice is readily available. Plants for bonsai work are chosen for several reasons; those most frequently used are, not surprisingly, natives of China and Japan. Although repeated pruning will reduce leaf size, it is advisable to choose species with naturally small leaves. The plants should also be able to survive for many years in a container, tolerating root pruning and consequent disturbances, as well as being able to thrive in the local conditions.

Acquiring Plants for Bonsai Work

Plants may be obtained from the wild, taking care not to violate any local restrictions, or grown from seed or purchased from a nursery. When buying from a nursery, a reputable bonsai grower and artist is preferable. With the increasing interest in Far Eastern cultures, there are merchants offering for sale plants which they refer to as 'bonsai', but which are, in reality, young plants which have been cut back, without any specialist knowledge of how and where to cut or any attempt being made to train them into shape. More detailed information on all aspects of bonsai may be found in specialist publications.

6

Water

Throughout Japanese history and culture water has been recognized as essential for all life, whether flora or fauna. Also seen as a symbol of a pure mind, body and spirit, water in some form, either real or representational, is fundamental to Japanese gardens and their design. The sight and sound of water, on whatever scale, has a calming influence, enhancing tranquillity and contemplation. In Japanese-style gardens water is featured in diverse ways which vary from a gentle trickle supplying a water basin or deer scarer, to large volumes flowing over waterfalls into ponds or lakes.

Water Basins

Even in the smallest space the sight and sound of flowing water can be enjoyed. Water basins (*chozubachi*), either standing alone or as part of a grouping, are traditionally placed near the entrance to a building or garden, often occupying a limited space next to a verandah or tea house. In the sixteenth century, with the development of tea gardens, water basins became an integral part of the ritual preparation for participation in the ceremony.

Typically water basins used in tea gardens are low in height so that all have to stoop to use the water, thereby being humbled, and all guests, of whatever social standing, become equal. The *chozubachi* is the main element of a *tsukubai* grouping, which traditionally also includes an assortment of stones (*yakuishi*), including three low, flat stones set to the front of the basin, one being large enough to stand or sit on safely. Of the other two, the one to the right was used for resting a container of hot water, the stone on the left was used to support a lantern for evening ceremonies. A fourth, larger, stone set behind the water basin balanced the grouping visually.

Where the water flows over the lip of the *chozubachi* or is splashed by participants, a 'sink' and a drain are provided, disguised by smaller, dark grey or black stones, most usually of a uniformly rounded shape which glisten when wet. In addition to the low tea garden *chozubachi*, there are various,

ABOVE:
Tsukubai *layout.*

OPPOSITE PAGE:
Copper, cupped 'rain chain'.
Private garden, Dorset, England.

Tall stone chozubachi *adjacent to verandah.*
Nishi-Hongan-ji Temple, Kyoto.

Kakei *and* chozubachi. *School courtyard*
garden, Hampshire, England.

somewhat taller styles used in free-standing situations, and taller still, those used adjacent to elevated verandahs.

Chozubachi are usually made from natural stone, popularly grey granite, and may be either recycled from other objects or hewn from quarried stone. Sometimes a suitably shaped stone may be adapted by carving out a reservoir and levelling the base.

In the earliest gardens, water would be directed along a channel, usually made of bamboo, into a long, thin bamboo spout (*kakei*), poised over the *chozubachi*, through which the water trickled into the basin. The flow continued after passing through the *tsukubai*, sometimes forming a stream or feeding a small pond with continuous fresh water. Today, it is unlikely that a fresh water supply will be available, and in modern installations water is recycled by using a submersible electric pump.

Kakei

Where cut bamboo is available and the site is appropriate, it is possible to make *kakei* in the original style. Alternatively, imported *kakei* are available in the West, usually consisting of an upright piece of bamboo, approximately 50mm (2in) in diameter and 1m (3ft) in height, secured into the ground and the top of which slots into a wooden block. Another, slightly smaller piece of bamboo is inserted into the block at an angle poised over the water basin. Internodes within the bamboo are punctured, forming a channel which houses a flexible feed pipe connected to the water supply and circulatory system.

Installing Chozubachi

The method of installing *chozubachi* will vary depending on the style and siting, but the basic principles are similar.

Natural stone *chozubachi*, particularly those made of granite, are heavy and need to be safely supported, either by imbedding in the ground or in a mortar base. When sited in the centre of a *tsukubai* grouping a watertight reservoir needs to be provided, together with a brick or stone supporting plinth.

Where preformed 'pebble ponds' are available, the *chozubachi* may either be sited on the edge of the reservoir or, by providing adequate support, such as flat, steel rods which straddle the pond, the water basin can be sited over the reservoir. A submersible pump, capable of raising water to the desired height to flow through the *kakei*, is placed in the reservoir and connected to the flexible water pipe. It is important

that all safety precautions are observed (*see* above). It is equally important to ensure that the water in the reservoir is at least sufficient to cover the pump adequately to avoid overheating and damage. Unless the water supply is controlled by a float valve or solenoid, levels will need to be checked regularly and topped up when necessary. The water spout will need to be securely installed in the correct position, either by concreting it into the ground (a disadvantage when replacement becomes necessary) or by slotting it into a subterranean waterproof pipe of a diameter larger than the upright of the *kakei*. Infilling with gravel provides stability.

Finally, the all-important water ladle, also contrived out of bamboo, is laid across the top of the basin, enabling all who pass to drink the refreshing and cleansing water. After this, the ladle is rinsed out by each participant and returned to its resting place, with the open end downwards. Sometimes the ladle is rested on short lengths of bamboo, tied together with black hemp.

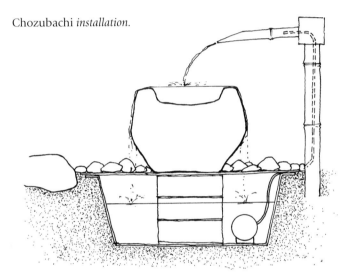

Chozubachi installation.

Suikinkutsu

The sound of water can be highlighted by the addition of an ingenious underground echo chamber – *suikinkutsu*. In Japan earthenware pots are made for this purpose. If imports are not available, it is fairly easy to adapt a large pot as a *suikinkutsu*. When using a pot made for plants, a drainage hole will already be provided in the base; a second hole is required near to the lip of the pot, into which a drainage pipe is fitted.

'Pebble pond' reservoir, with steel supporting bar for chozubachi. School courtyard garden, Hampshire, England.

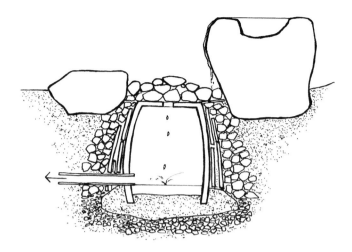

Suikinkutsu *installation.*

Shishi-odoshi. *Exhibition garden, Birmingham, England.*

A pit will need to be prepared in front of the *chozubachi* at the place where the overflowing water hits the ground. The depth of the pit is calculated so that the finished height of the *suikinkutsu* will be level with the ground surface. The bottom of the pit is lined with gravel and the upturned pot is set in cement. When pressing the rim of the pot into the wet cement, check the levels. Connect the drainage pipe and seal. Ideally, the pot should be protected by a layer of curved tiles, followed by stones or rubble and finally backfilling with soil. Following the completion of the *suikinkutsu*, the *chozubachi* and the associated stone placings may be installed.

Shishi-odoshi

The earliest *shishi-odoshi* (bird, deer or boar scarers) were designed by farmers to keep predators away from their crops by using materials which were readily available. *Shishi-odoshi* are therefore most usually constructed from bamboo and wood. Water, originally obtained from natural streams, trickles through a thin bamboo pipe into a larger piece of bamboo which is set at an angle on a wooden axle. The first internode is removed, but all the others are left intact. As the water builds up, the hollow bamboo begins to pivot downwards and eventually the weight of water pushes the tip so far that the water empties, and the now heavier sealed end of the bamboo drops backwards suddenly, striking a strategically placed stone and making a sharp, rhythmical, clacking sound. The water drains into a 'sink' covered in pebbles, and nowadays will inevitably be recycled by a submersible pump. A solar-powered pump is an advantage here as the clacking

sound will automatically stop after dark. Due to the fact that *shishi-odoshi* were developed in rural areas, their use in a garden hints at the countryside, and for preference they are placed near to hedges or country-style plantings. Alternatively, a *shishi-odoshi* is useful beside a pond to scare predatory herons away from valuable and tempting fish.

Rain Chains

A Japanese flavour can be introduced on a modest scale by the installation of 'rain chains' (*kusari-doi*). Rain chains replace the customary Western way of channelling the run-off from roofs through a downpipe into the drainage system. When chains or a system of 'cups' are used instead of the downpipe, rain water is usually directed through an under-eaves channel to an opening which, in turn, carries it to the chain. The sight of water sparkling and dancing as it trickles down the chain is restful and contemplative.

As it is important to keep any splashing water away from the fabric of the building, the installation of rain chains or cups is particularly appropriate and easily achieved when there is an overhanging roof, as in much Japanese and some Western architecture. Rain chains may still be used even if there is no overhang by contriving a means of extending it away from the building.

In Japan rain chains and cups vary from the very humble to imposing features. There are several designs of chains, usually made of aluminium or stainless steel, sometimes plastic. Similarly, there are varying designs of cups, some of which are fairly plain, others having more decorative finishes. Traditionally, cups have been made of copper and hang from ornate 'hoppers'. They are now also available in plastic, which is lighter in weight and less costly.

Imported rain chains and cups of authentic design are now readily available in the West. When choosing, it is necessary to ensure that a sufficient length for the drop from the eave height to ground level has been allowed for. When it is possible, it is advisable to purchase the custom-made weights which are attached to the bottom of the chains and keep the whole vertically straight.

Installing Kusari-doi

Installation is very straightforward. Depending on whether water is carried by an under-eaves channel or along guttering, the chains or cups can simply be hung through the

Rain chain.
Suzaku no Niwa, Kyoto.

Cupped 'rain chain'.
Nikko.

opening, suspended either from a nail or by using stiff wire bent into a triangular shape, which can be threaded through one end of the chain and pinched together to pass through the opening in the guttering or channel. On releasing it, the wire springs back and holds the chain in place.

Wells

Early Japanese settlements arose near to natural water sources, rivulets tumbling down the hillsides, rivers, wells or ponds. With the development of the tea garden (*roji*) the concept of cleansing water was woven into their design. Clean water was, and is, clearly vital for the making of high-quality tea. A well would be an important feature within a garden, located on the way to the tea house; sometimes the bench where guests relax and wait to be summoned to the ceremony is sited near to a well.

Although fresh water may no longer be readily available, it is still customary to include the notion of collectible fresh water by including a well-head in the garden. The style and materials used for making them vary; some are wooden, with a thatched or shingled roof, from which is suspended the bucket and lifting apparatus. The raising and the lowering of the bucket are similar to the operation of a block and tackle, with the rope being fed through the 'block', which is sometimes ceramic but, more usually, wooden.

To imply the availability of fresh water, simpler well-heads are often included as a feature in domestic gardens. In the West it is possible to obtain imported, carved, granite well-heads, which are held in position on a mortar bed. Instead of a roof, a simple bamboo covering which can be rolled back or removed is laid over the top of the 'well'.

Well and covered gateway.
Omote Senke School of Tea, Kyoto.

Onsen

In common with all archipelagos, the islands of Japan are volcanic in origin; numerous volcanoes are potentially active and erupt unpredictably and there is a constant threat of earthquakes, some on a small scale, others resulting in national disasters. Heat generated by so much volcanic activity near to the surface is manifested in widespread hot springs and ponds.

Traditionally, the Japanese have bathed in the steaming waters in all weathers, including the depth of winter when outside temperatures are frequently well below freezing and heavy falls of snow are commonplace. Many spa towns have grown around the hot water springs, together with hotels and baths which have diverted the healing waters into

indoor facilities, some very select. Even in small hotels or guest houses a hot water bath (*onsen*) is provided for guests, sometimes using natural hot spring water but, increasingly, heated domestic water is all that is available. Where possible, hot water baths are located in the part of a building where bathers can overlook a natural mountain scene or a tranquil garden. In cold weather the wall of glass remains closed, in warmer weather it can be rolled back like a screen so that bath and garden can be enjoyed to the full.

Onsen may also be enjoyed as an integral part of a garden. They may be made from natural stone, in a pond-like construction with the hot water tumbling over a stone waterfall. A less complicated alternative is a wooden tub for a domestic *onsen*, which may be small enough for one person to enjoy or large enough for several to gather together. Where it is desirable, a protective roof of rice straw, wooden shingles or split bamboo may be provided. A water heater with a

Installing teak onsen. *Private garden, Dorset, England.*

BELOW: *Waterfall and 'carp' stone. Ginkaku-ji Temple, Kyoto.*

timer may be sited near to the *onsen* to heat the water to be ready for use at a predetermined time. However, if it is preferable for the water to be maintained at a high temperature for use at any time it is important to retain the heat with an easily removable, insulated cover. In the garden the *onsen* can be installed above ground and provided with access steps and possibly a platform. When it is sunk below ground level access for maintenance becomes more difficult, but the installation is less obtrusive within the garden.

It should be noted that, when using any hot water bathing facility in Japan, bodily cleansing takes place before one enters the bath or *onsen* and the hot water thus remains pleasant for others to enjoy. The grime of the day is washed away, usually under a conventional shower which drains into a foul water system and the cleansed bathers relax in the hot water, admiring the garden and listening to the birds singing and the water flowing.

Waterfalls

The design and construction of waterfalls in Japanese gardens has traditionally copied early Chinese and Japanese landscape paintings depicting rugged mountains with deep, mysterious crevasses, through which water finds its way, falling towards rivers, lakes and the sea. As well as invoking a natural scene, waterfalls (*taki*) may be deeply symbolic. Taoism and Shintoism, believed that the gods inhabited water and endowed waterfalls and associated rocks with

Nuno-ochi (Fabric fall).

Ito-ochi (Ribbon fall).

Tsutai-ochi (Curtain falls).

Kasane-ochi (Tiered falls).

Types of waterfalls.

spirituality, identifying them with rice straw or paper garlands. Buddhist beliefs may also be incorporated in waterfall design, by choosing and placing the most significant stones to represent the Buddhist trilogy of Buddha and his two attendants. Falls constructed in this way are always higher than the norm, reaching anything up to 6m (18ft).

At the foot of the fall may be placed a 'carp' stone, perpetuating a Chinese legend which tells of a river with a three-tiered waterfall; if a fish proved strong and determined enough to swim to the top of the falls, it would be transformed into a dragon. In Zen Buddhism this reaffirms man's struggle for enlightenment through triumph over adversity. Similarly, a flatter, wider stone can be set at the foot of the falls to provide a 'splash' stone which breaks up the flow and enhances the sound of moving water.

There are several styles of waterfall typical of Japanese gardens, each with characteristic stone placings directing the water to create various effects. The classification of waterfalls depends on the number and style of the cascades. The twelfth-century *Book of the Garden*, the *Sakuteiki*, details several 'manners of falling', describing the choice and placing of stones: the linen falling or veil-like falls (*nuno-ochi*) consists of a single, wide flow of water cascading over a flat stone, preferably with an interesting front surface; to create this curtain effect it may be necessary to dam the running water at the top of the fall so that it flows gently over the lip of the stone. The thread falling or ribbon falls (*ito-ochi*) is created by placing an upright stone with a jagged edge at the top of the falls, which directs the flowing water into several separate falls, giving the appearance of hanging threads. In the running falls (*tsutai-ochi*) rocks are so arranged that the water trickles down the face of the rocks, instead of making a free-flowing fall. To make tiered falls (*kasane-ochi*) the water is directed into falls of different widths and heights by the placing of assorted rocks to provide the variability.

Where possible, it is desirable to site waterfalls to face towards the moon, so that the reflection of the moonlight on the falling water can be enjoyed.

Building Waterfalls

In Japanese-style gardens, waterfalls, almost inevitably, flow into a pond or stream. The materials excavated to form the pond or watercourse are used to create the 'hillside' for the waterfall. For a large project, particularly when using mechanical diggers, it is advisable, as the work proceeds, to place the excavated materials in a preliminary shape which roughly resembles the finished design. Unless limited by space, it is preferable that the hillside should be constructed to allow for a header pool from which the circulating water flows over the falls. As rocks of varying weights and sizes will be arranged to create the style of the falls, it is important that the hillside be

Waterfall flowing into artificial lake.
Kyoto Garden, Holland Park, London, England.

whole system is watertight, either by the use of butyl or other liners, as well as waterproofed and sealed mortar. Unless a natural source of flowing water is available, provision needs to be made for the installation of a circulating pump at an early stage. For a small project, a submersible pump can be placed at the foot of the falls, with a return to the header pond. The pump must be capable of raising the volume of water to the required height. It will also be necessary to install filters of the appropriate capacity, particularly where foliage and plant debris will fall into the water, and especially when koi carp are kept in the pond or stream. In installations where large volumes of water are being moved, it is advisable to construct a separate pumping station, so that the controls are within reach for any adjustments and all equipment is accessible for maintenance. Siting the pump at a level below the main reservoir ensures that, by gravity feeding, the pump will not dry out. It is useful too to incorporate a means of diverting water from the main flow, particularly during maintenance, utilizing the pump to drain water from the pond or stream.

Plants to Complement Waterfalls

During the installation of the natural stones, planting pockets should be allowed for, incorporating a good quality planting medium. Bear in mind that most plants in Japanese gardens prefer an acidic soil.

The choice of plants will vary depending on the style of the whole garden, the size of the waterfall and its siting; typically, ornamental maples (*momiji*) will overhang the upper reaches of the falls, forming a visual framework, complemented by evergreen *Pieris* spp., evergreen azaleas, ferns, and low-growing 'pines', such as *Pinus mugo* 'Gnom' or *Chamaecyparis obtusa* 'Nana Gracilis'. As with all plantings in a Japanese-style garden, it is quality not quantity that is important.

stable and able to carry the weight of rocks, mortar and water. It is advisable too to provide an adequate supporting structure of bricks or concrete blocks, which will be camouflaged when the natural rocks are *in situ*.

Having decided on the style of the falls and prepared drawings for it, to choose rocks of the desired quality and shape is an important and enjoyable step, envisaging how they will be sited. All the rocks should be of the same type, as they would be in a natural environment and, when placed in position, should appear as though they had tumbled there naturally.

The *Sakuteiki* gives clear guidelines in 'The Procedure for Making the Waterfall', which includes the order of installing the stones, beginning at the bottom and working upwards. Stones should be set firmly in place, filling all the openings between them with a mortar mix which includes waterproofing additives. In constructing all the parts where water will lie, flow or splash it is important to ensure that the

Streams

The movement of water through a garden has been deeply rooted in Japanese garden design over many centuries and encompassing changing philosophies and styles. Water courses may vary from a slow, shallow trickle emanating from a *chozubachi* or *shishi-odoshi*, to a broad, deep flow resembling a natural stream. As with waterfalls, unless a natural stream runs through the garden, the choice of design will depend on the style and size of the whole garden, the location of the stream and the available budget.

Ideally, in deference to the belief that the power of the eastern Blue Dragon would drive out the evils that may be

blocking the way of the western White Tiger, a stream should flow from the north-eastern corner towards the south, turning to the west, as in the *shinden*-style gardens developed in the Heian period. However, this is not always possible.

Trickling Streams

When creating a modest, trickling stream, the stream bed can be shallow, 15 to 20cm (6–8in) in depth, with rounded pebbles of differing size laid along the bottom, resulting in a natural appearance and creating breaks in the flow which sparkle in sunlight. The edges of a shallow stream may be defined with either larger natural pebbles set in mortar or with subtle plantings which may be simply of grass or a low-growing ground cover such as *Soleirolia soleirolii* or *Ophiopogon* 'Tamaryu', neither of which needs mowing, thus reducing the maintenance and possible problems caused by lawn mowings.

The *Sakuteiki* recommends that 'the ratio of the drop of elevation to the distance of the running stream be three to one hundred', which represents the native decimal system of measurement. It goes on to say that 'the stream will flow smoothly with a murmuring sound'.

Winding Streams

Since the Heian period (794–1185) winding streams have been those most popularly recreated in a garden setting. In designing such a stream, to achieve the most authentic appearance it is important to observe how the flow of water interacts with the terrain through which it passes. Water will find the easiest way to reach its goal, consequently undermining banks which are of soft or sandy material, flowing around hard rocks and accelerating through narrow gorges and crevasses. Depending on the structure of the banks, flowing water generally erodes the bank at the base of an outside curve. A hard stone set slightly away from the bank will deflect the flow of water, giving protection to vulnerable areas. When designing a winding stream, the inclusion of stones which redirect the flow also enhances its natural appearance. Other, randomly placed stones breaking the surface of the water will create interesting eddies and further alterations in the flow. Under some conditions naturally flowing water forms gently sloping shorelines or beaches on the inside of bends in the stream. Throughout the long history of Japanese garden design, stone 'beaches' have been included in the shorelines of winding streams, as well as at the edges of ponds, adding to the naturalness of their appearance. 'Beaches' also provide a pedestrian access point, enabling visitors to view the water, stones and plantings more closely.

Plantings Associated with Winding Streams

Plantings associated with winding streams are chosen with care. A few windswept pines along the shoreline suggest a barren, mountainous landscape. Gently sloping grassy banks, with the occasional well-placed rock and accent plant, indicate a calm, pastoral scene. Maples overhanging a rocky shoreline hint of the countryside. Sometimes stones are represented by heavily pruned box, *Buxus microphylla japonica* or evergreen

azaleas. In slow running, clear water, irises may flourish. *Iris kaempferi*, syn *I. ensata* which flowers in May and June, rises gently above the glassy surface. Irises may be planted direct into the stream floor, or into baskets especially made for aquatic plants. In wide streams, rectangular, wooden planting boxes prevent the planting medium from crumbling into the water, and keep the plantings contained.

Another, often-used technique for containing iris plantings, particularly at the edge of a pond, is to form a barrier with hardwood posts set vertically and closely together, their tops slightly higher than the surface of the pond.

Construction of Streams

When the style and the size of the stream have been decided, the limits need to be marked out on the ground, making allowances for bends and changing widths. The channel is then dug either by hand or mechanically, ensuring that there is sufficient fall from top to bottom. If powered equipment is used for any excavations in a garden, it is important to balance its value in terms of time and labour against the possible damage it may cause through the compaction of the soil, especially where there will be plantings. When powered equipment is the chosen option, it is important to remove the topsoil and keep it separate. At all times the weight of the machinery should be distributed on substantial planks or boards. A circulating pump and its associated pipework will need to be installed in the early stages of construction.

Providing a watertight lining for the stream is imperative. The most flexible method is to use purpose-made butyl, which moulds into the excavated shape. It is advisable to provide a cushioning bed for the liner to prevent damage by rocks and stones. Cushioning may be either by layers of newspaper, a purpose-made protective matting or a layer of soft sand. Where it is necessary to use several pieces of butyl, lay the lowest piece first, overlapping subsequent pieces, working upwards. Seal the joints with a waterproof contact adhesive or cold-weld tape. At the edges of the stream form a trench into which the butyl is laid. The trench may eventually be filled with topsoil, a planting medium or randomly placed rocks set in mortar. In any event, the edges of the liner need to be firmly fixed and well covered to prevent deterioration caused by ultraviolet light, as well as to create a more natural effect. The fixing of the edges should not be completed until the stream has been filled with water, since the weight of the water will pull the liner into any air pockets and uneven surfaces, subsequently dragging down the edges of the liner. To disguise the liner in the stream bed distribute a mixture of water-washed pebbles of at least 15mm (0.6in) diameter, which can be removed in the event of any repairs becoming necessary. A stream can also be lined with waterproofed concrete, which may have a longer life than a

butyl liner, but its installation will be more costly and less flexible, resulting in a more artificial appearance.

Ponds

In addition to the historical and spiritual origins of ponds in Japanese gardens which have been described earlier, aesthetically the horizontal surface of a pond, of any size, complements the surrounding verticals of hillsides and associated plantings. Reflected images of the environs are particular features of bodies of water in Japanese gardens.

The free-form shapes and sizes are chosen to be in harmony with the whole garden setting. It is important to consider the capacity of the water available either from a natural source or via a circulatory system which also services any falls or associated watercourses. Measurements will also depend on whether there will be aquatic plants in the water or around the pond edges and whether koi carp will be there. When planning a pond for koi consideration needs to be given to their natural habitat and feeding habits. The primary motivation for keeping them is to enjoy their movement through the water and their individual markings. Bear in mind that koi are bottom feeders and unless the deeper water to the centre of the pond is crystal clear, sightings will be limited. Creating a shallower area on the periphery of the pond will overcome this limitation. Even in very small spaces it is usual to include a viewing place at the water's edge from where visitors can tempt the fish to come closer by offering food.

Pond Construction

The excavation for a manmade pond will need to be carefully planned, taking into account the possibly large volume of material that will need to be moved. If a 'pond and hill' feature is planned, it will be necessary to consider the eventual overall shape and depth of the pond, as well as the basis for the hill and waterfall. It may be possible to undertake smaller projects manually, with the assistance of a wheelbarrow. Larger projects will probably be manageable only with a mechanical digger. Similar limitations and possible problems apply as for creating a stream channel, and the digger operator will need to be in tune with the designer to create the required differences in levels and free-flowing shapes, and to bear in mind any rocks which have been selected for the final set piece. Traditionally, pond linings were of compacted, hard clay, but now it is simpler to use a custom-made, butyl liner. Liners are available in a variety of thicknesses and widths and are usually sold from a roll. For larger ponds it may be necessary to find a specialist supplier who will probably have a bigger choice of sizes and thicknesses than the local garden centre. When calculating the required size of the liner, measure the maximum diameter, add to it twice the maximum depth plus allowances for extending the liner beyond the pond perimeter into a surrounding trench. Additional allowance will also need to be made for any longer, gentler slopes, such as are required when creating a pebble beach. The liner must always extend above the waterline, and design detail is important to ensure that it is hidden.

To preserve the butyl liner from damage, a protective underlay needs to be provided. There are several methods recommended; however, the current thinking is that a layer of cushioning underlay will suffice. As with the stream bed preparation, the underlay may be several thicknesses of newspaper, old carpeting or a purpose-made matting. The calculations for its sizing will be the same as for the butyl liner.

To prevent the formation of air pockets during the installation, it is advisable to fill the pond partly with water so that its weight levels out any undulations in the liner and the underlay. Before fixing the edges, the pond should be filled as deeply as possible without hindering the installation of any edging stones.

When choosing rocks or boulders to edge a pond, bear in mind that asymmetry is the aim and that uniform materials are unwelcome. To install the rocks, a ledge which will be below the finished water level is formed. To ensure greater stability, a waterproofed concrete footing can be laid along the ledge underneath the liner. The natural rocks, which will protrude above the final water level, are set randomly around the ledge, some in front of others and some higher than others to give a more natural finish. It may be that some larger, flatter stones are positioned as viewing platforms, all secured in place with waterproofed cement.

Where the pond design includes details such as stepping stones, bridges or islands, the liner will need to be protected from possible puncturing by hard materials. This can be done by laying reinforcing wire or steel mesh on top of the liner, taking care that the reinforcing material does not puncture the liner. Cover with 50–100mm (2–4in) of mortar of a consistency that can be spread smoothly; finally apply a sealant.

If it is proposed to introduce plants at the water margins, ledges of sufficient size to hold planting baskets securely will need to be included in the contouring before the liners are laid.

Installing butyl liner and selecting edging stones.
Private garden, Hampshire, England.

Lysichiton camtschatcensis.
Nikko Botanical Garden, Nikko.

Plantings Associated with Ponds

Ornamental plantings in and around ponds in Japanese gardens usually follow the customary low-key style. After irises, the most frequently planted aquatics are *Nelumbo nucifera* or sacred lotus, which bears large leaves on long stalks held above water. In summer, the single or double, creamy-white or pink flowers rise above the leaf canopy. Before the flowers open, distinctive pointed buds appear. The flat-topped seed pods are used in oriental cuisine and, when dried, in flower arrangements. Although reputed to be frost-hardy, the lotus prefers a subtropical or tropical climate.

For ponds in which koi are to be kept the choice of plants is limited. Koi feed on and uproot most plant materials but do not damage some species with surface foliage such as *Nelumbo* spp., under which the fish find shade on hot, sunny days. In cooler climates, more reliable aquatic plants are *Nymphaea* spp., water lily, which has a growth habit somewhat different to *Nelumbo*. *Nymphaea* foliage rests on or near to the water surface and the starlike flowers are held slightly above the foliage. Flower colours vary from white to dark red, with some yellows and blues.

Recommended only for the edges of larger ponds is *Lysichiton camtschatcensis*, white skunk cabbage, an herbaceous perennial bearing rosettes of large, strongly veined, leathery leaves. In summer it produces large, upright white spathes with an unpleasant smell.

'Dry' Water (*Kare-Sansui*)

The origins of using hard materials to represent water have been described earlier, and, although the philosophical and spiritual aspects are similar, there are some subtle differences in design styles.

The early *kare-sansui* gardens were built in the precincts of Zen temples, most notably in Kyoto where the readily available Shirakawa gravel, derived from weathered granite, was most usually used. Many of these gardens were associated with the abbot's quarters (*hojo*), where scholars could meditate and contemplate the scene. As the gardens bordered straight-sided buildings and were usually contained within a walled boundary, the available spaces were frequently rectangular and of varying size. The borders retaining the loose aggregates were typically lengths of cut, grey granite of appropriate proportions. Where the garden was adjacent to a building, a drainage channel containing pebbles would take away the rain falling from the overhanging tile or shingle roof.

Kare-sansui inevitably portrayed a legendary or philosophical belief (*see* Chapter 2) and were a vehicle for releasing the mind from everyday matters and achieving an inner peace. Gardens similarly styled can be a restful part of a domestic garden and evoke those same images and responses.

'Dry' Waterfalls (Kare-Taki)

The implications of a natural water source flowing from a dark, mystical canyon, using rocks and pebbles, were first exploited in the latter part of the Muromachi period, and their construction continues into the present.

Despite there not being the pleasurable sound of flowing water, a dry waterfall can give a powerful impression of the real thing and at the same time hint that water has flowed there in the past and may do so again in the future. Dry waterfalls are less complicated to build than those with running water and do not need the pumps, filters and other equipment essential for them; in consequence costs and maintenance are substantially reduced. *Kare-taki* may be successfully built in gardens where the introduction of water would be difficult or too expensive. They can also be of a style and dimensions in balance with the whole garden

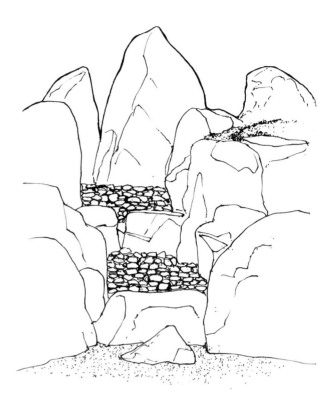

Kare-taki, *Tiger Glen Garden.*
Nishi-hongan-ji Temple, Kyoto.

Multi-tiered dry waterfall.

BELOW: *Preliminary stages of setting stones for*
kare-taki. *Private garden, Hampshire, England.*

whether it is small or large, and are often constructed in a corner of the site. The styles of *kare-taki* may be similar to those of waterfalls, such as single- or multi-tiered, or allude to rapids in a fast-flowing river.

To choose stones for the larger, mostly vertical, elements of a *kare-taki* follows guidelines similar to those for natural waterfalls: envisaging how the rocks will be sited and selecting those of the same geological type. Installation is more straightforward than for running water since waterproofing is unnecessary, and any supporting structures will be less complicated.

'Dry' Streams

As with natural waterfalls, *kare-taki* may flow into a dry stream or pond. Materials used in the dry stream may be a

Dry stream. Daitoku-ji *Temple complex, Kyoto.*

'Dry' Ponds

The illusion of a rippling pond can be created on any scale. A dry pond may be part of a larger, dry waterfall and stream composition, or it may stand alone. *Kare-sansui* gardens may be of any size, depending on the space available; they are particularly effective in small courtyards where growing plants and the maintaining of clear running water may be problematical. In a domestic setting they can be of a free-form shape or have rectangular boundaries. It may be that a major part of the horizontal surface is gravelled, perhaps with islands, sometimes connected by a stone bridge and sometimes with carefully selected plantings, usually forming a vertical contrast to the dry pond. In domestic gardens the gravelled area is more likely to be a part of the whole design, as a natural water pond would be, bounded by moss or '*tamaryu*' plantings. The gravel may be held in place by an edging of natural stones or granite setts, which also provide an interface between the loose materials and the peripheral plantings. In Western gardens this is particularly useful when there is grass which needs to be regularly mown, since gravel chippings can seriously damage mower blades and even be deflected to cause damage to any nearby glass doors or windows or to anyone in the line of fire.

Choosing Materials

When choosing stone for a *kare-sansui* garden it is important to find materials which most closely resemble those used in authentic Japanese gardens. Natural products are preferable, although it is now possible to find cast concrete slabs containing fragments of granite or other appropriate materials which are acceptable for paved areas. Granite blocks may sometimes be found in reclamation yards, and natural stone monoliths may be available from a local stone merchant or direct from quarries.

The choice of gravels or small stones will be those which closely replicate those found in Japan, most often in subdued shades of greyish white; for more modern styles a brownish colour is also appropriate. Choose a gravel that does not show dirt, is a uniform size of 5–12mm (about ½in or smaller) and does not break easily. A hard material is preferable since softer stones will create their own dust and have a dull appearance.

Installing Dry Gardens

To install a dry garden, the levels need to be reduced to an appropriate depth below the finished surface which, in turn, will depend on the method of construction. It has long been recommended that a concrete base should be prepared and

continuation of those used to represent water in the *kare-taki* or they may become a blend of different pebbles, arranged to resemble the randomly tumbled, rounded stones often found in a dry river bed. In a more stylized format, slate 'paddlestones' are methodically laid in the dry stream bed, beginning at the point furthest from the source and working backwards, slightly overlaying each one in a fish scale pattern, giving a finished appearance of flowing water.

The construction and maintenance of a dry stream is also less complicated and more economical than for a similarly sized wet stream since it is obviously not necessary to provide a circulating system or a waterproof stream bed, and the removal of plant debris is also simpler, particularly in the autumn. Another advantage is that dry streams do not need a fall in level, a prerequisite for flowing water.

include a drainage system so that weeds are discouraged and the gravel does not hold puddles. However, a simpler and less expensive method is to firm the native soil, either by treading or with a mechanical vibrating 'plate', covering the whole with a semi-permeable membrane which prevents weed growth but allows water to drain through, and finishing with a 75mm (3in) layer of the chosen aggregate. When hard edges are part of the design these need to be concreted into place, pointed and allowed to dry before the aggregate is laid. For preference, the colour of pointing material should be complementary to the chosen edging.

If any rocks, stepping stones or bridges are part of the design these should be fixed in place before the gravel is laid. Any

plantings will need to be undertaken before the ground is prepared for the stonework, ensuring that adequately sized holes are dug and all plants provided with a good quality planting medium. The level of the top of the root ball should be set just below the finished level of the aggregate.

To create the raked patterns, it is necessary to have a heavy-duty rake specially made for the purpose. After having levelled the gravel, push the rake into the surface, forming ridges by stepping backwards and pulling the rake through. Traditionally raked patterns follow certain guidelines, which are recognized variously as ripples, streams, waves, eddies and the like. A gentle sprinkling of water will wash off any dirt.

Kare-sansui. *Dartington Hall, Devon, England.*

Installing stepping stones and granite bridge on semi-permeable membrane before laying pearly quartz. Private garden, Dorset, England.

7

Structural Features

The first impressions of Japanese gardens, of whatever style or period, can mislead the viewer into thinking that the primary components are the plantings and their management, stone used in several ways, including water basins – *chozubachi*, and lanterns – *toro*, water, either natural or representational, and the boundaries, whether they be fences, walls, plantings or a combination of materials. The very essence of many of the gardens of Japan, also depends on complementary structures, some of which form the framework for the garden setting, such as shrines, temples, palaces and dwelling houses; in addition, more modest structures form an integral part of garden design and ambience.

Outside Japan, especially in Western cultures, the replication of shrines and temples of a scale and grandeur equalling the traditional complexes and buildings is almost unknown, probably principally due to their association with Shintoism and Buddhism, in part due to the range of materials and skills necessary to complete such undertakings and in part to the prohibitive costs involved. Consequently, the backdrop of long, low, wooden buildings, with raised verandahs from which to view the gardens is rare in the West. Also rare is the accompanying magnificence of mud walls and imposing gateways.

Dwelling Houses

Similarly, dwelling houses built in traditional Japanese styles are also rare in the West, although in some circumstances it is possible to make adaptations which introduce a Japanese atmosphere. Where the dwelling is brick-built, a colour-washed rendering can be applied to resemble the traditional mud walls. If there is access from the building to the garden, a skilled craftsman could be employed to construct sliding doors. It is feasible to substitute rice paper for sand-blasted glass panels, but glass is not only more weatherproof, it also provides better security and is more likely to comply with local building regulations. The opening for sliding doors is centrally placed, with recessed finger holds for pulling back

Tsubo niwa, *viewed from above.*
Guest house, Kyoto.

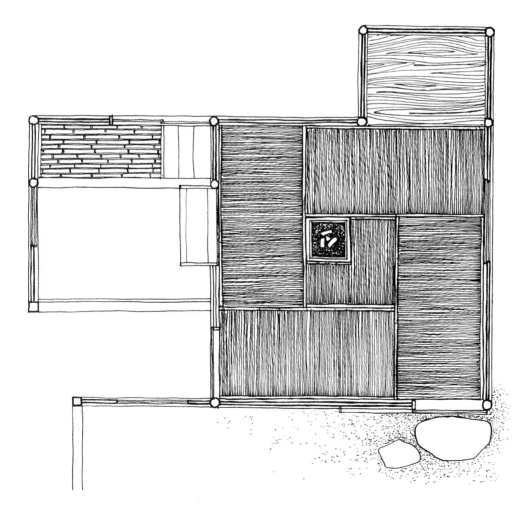

Plan of four-and-a-half tatami mat
tea house layout.

the doors. Where there are Western-style windows over-looking a Japanese-style garden, it may be possible to attach removable wooden grilles of appropriate design to the outside wall, giving the appearance of a traditional building.

Many old Japanese town houses were of timber construction, with narrow street frontages on deep plots. Integral parts of the layout of such houses often included a small courtyard overlooked from the raised building. Originally designed to bring light into the living areas, open spaces within the building became places in which small gardens could be accommodated and viewed from within the building, or provided pedestrian access from one building to another. The measurements for constructing houses were, and still are, largely based on sizes of the floor matting – *tatami*, which is a rigid mat constructed from stiff rice-straw, with a thin woven reed cover and a cloth tape binding. *Tatami* measure approximately 910mm × 1,820 mm (3ft × 6ft), and are laid in set formations in numbers usually varying from three upwards. Consequently, the open spaces within the building complex in which a garden could be created, would also be related to mat sizes, and maybe as small as one *tatami*. These gems of garden creation – *tsubo* – could only be enjoyed by those who had access to the dwelling. The tending of *tsubo* gardens was and is an important component of the daily life of the household, the energy invested in their care being returned in the form of re-energizing enjoyment.

Tea Houses

A uniquely Japanese structure, the tea house, is also based on *tatami* mat sizes. The building of replica tea houses may be a more viable proposition in the West, due to their smaller dimensions and the materials used. However, the accurate inclusion of the detail and symbolism woven into their design may be achieved only by trained designers and craftsman. Contrary to some Western misconceptions, the design of tea houses, which was developed by the tea masters of the sixteenth century, was based on modest farmhouses and remote, rustic hermitages, the materials used for the main structure suggesting that the timber had been gathered from nearby woods, and stones for the pathways and mud for the walls from in and around streams. Interiors resembled a humble and simple farmhouse with little natural light.

Although tea houses were designed to imitate rustic retreats, their early owners tended to be merchants who exhibited their aesthetic appreciation and wealth by selecting the best quality clay and sand mixes for the walls, and carefully choosing branches for the supporting structure which had the required elegance of shape and colour, and accepting only the finest, blemish-free timber for the roofing slats and window frames.

The most usual dimensions for a classic tea room is four-and-a-half *tatami* mats, or approximately 2,750mm square (9ft square), which accommodates up to five people. Four mats are arranged around the half mat which is in the middle of the room and includes the hearth. Over the hearth hangs a metal pot containing the water for the elaborate ceremony.

Some tea houses may be adjuncts to the main dwelling house, but more commonly are separate buildings, approached via the tea garden – *roji*. Guests entering the tea house do so by crawling through a door, *nijiri-guchi*, raised above the ground and level with the tea room floor. Guests participating in the early tea ceremonies were probably clad in either cumbersome samurai costumes or restrictive kimonos for the ladies. To aid their negotiation of the *nijiri-guchi*, a large, raised stepping stone would be placed in front of the small entrance. Once inside the tea room, which is typically enclosed on all four sides, the semi-darkness hints

Rustic tea house.
Kenrokuen garden, Kanazawa.

at remoteness and humility, isolating the mind from all external influences and encouraging a return to simple values, spiritual awareness and enlightenment.

To design and construct a tea house it is recommended that reference should be made to specialist books which give dimensions, materials and other details. Some considered poetic licence may be acceptable in choosing substitute materials, such as replacing the clay and sand walls with waterproof boarding, which can be treated to give a roughened surface appearance and colour-washed with a sandy/clay-coloured masonry paint. Where *tatami* mats are not available, sprung floor boarding may be the optimal alternative. It is important at all times to retain the natural, rustic and secluded appearance.

Waiting Benches

En route to the tea house there will often be a waiting bench, on which guests can rest, dispel the pressures of the day and prepare themselves for participation in the ceremony. As with tea houses, waiting benches were fashioned from natural materials, giving the impression of a modest, rustic structure, made from the materials close at hand: clay walls on two or three sides, supported by vertically set, natural logs which, in turn, carry the supporting framework for a roof finished with cedar shingles, thatch or bamboo. Even though the aim is for an informal appearance, much of the structure, especially the roof is painstakingly and meticulously crafted.

On one of the long sides of the covered bench, wooden seating is provided. The approach to the bench is typically a digression from the main stepping-stone path. Frequently a *tsukubai* grouping of water basin and ladle, with accompanying lantern, would be adjacent to the waiting bench to provide guests with cleansing and purifying water. Sometimes an earthen closet would be an integral part of the bench structure or be a separate hut nearby, ensuring that guests were comfortable before entering the tea house for a ceremony that might last for anything up to four hours.

Garden Viewing and Resting Benches

Within some strolling gardens there may be a covered bench where visitors can rest. Unlike tea garden waiting benches, strolling garden benches are inwardly facing, enabling comfortable conversation. Most often, the roof shape will be round, hexagonal or square, supported by evenly spaced

Waiting bench.
Omote Senke School of Tea, Kyoto.

wooded posts and usually finished with thatch or cedar shingles. The 'walls' are only as high as the low backs of the benches, so that visitors can enjoy the garden viewed through and framed by the spaces above. To provide a prime view of the garden, the bench may be raised on a plinth or set at the top of a hill.

Although the design of a strolling garden bench is different from that of a tea garden bench, similar materials are used to achieve a natural appearance. Here too, the meticulous attention to detail in construction can readily be seen, particularly in the roof framework.

During the Heian period, when grandiose pond and island gardens were created and boating parties abounded, covered benches were often built on islands from which guests could view and enjoy the colourful passing boats, listen to the music and recite poetry. Visitors would be ferried to the island and disembark on to a landing stage, on the way to the viewing bench. Such benches would be of a more formal style and face towards the water.

Bridges (*Hashi*)

The concept of crossing water by boat does not easily come to mind when thinking of Japanese-style gardens. However, bridges of varying styles have long been associated with them. In addition to the practicality of crossing water with ease, there is the symbolism associated with the transition from one world to another. A strong feature of the eleventh-century garden of Byodo-in in Uji is the wooden bridge which symbolizes man's passage from worldly cares to the 'Pure Land' paradise of Amida Buddha.

Garden viewing/resting bench.
Heian Shrine garden, Kyoto.

Covered Bridges

Substantial bridges were designed and installed in many important gardens through the centuries, some of which were covered with intricate roofs. In the garden of the Shugaku-in Imperial Villa, on the north-eastern outskirts of Kyoto, is *Chisote-bashi*, 'The Bridge of a Thousand Years', which joins two islands. Built in 1824, one large stone slab spans the water, supported by two cut stone piers. A roofed corridor passes between the two major parts of the bridge. On top of the roof of the eastern pier sits a gilded copper phoenix, and the western pier has a hipped roof and bench seating for visitors to sit and admire the water beneath.

Constructed during the Meiji period in 1895, the Heian shrine garden in Kyoto also has a distinctive, partly covered, bridge. The span of the bridge is in a traditional wooden design, with an 'eyebrow'-shaped, thatched roof towards the middle. Under the roof are seating benches which protrude over the water and provide a resting place and vantage point for viewing the nearby islands and the colourful koi gliding through the water.

ABOVE: Chisote-bashi. *Shugaku-in, Imperial Villa garden, Kyoto.*

LEFT: Covered bridge.
Heian Shrine garden, Kyoto.

ABOVE: Traditional curved bridge.
Ritsurin Koen, Takamatsu.

LEFT: Rustic bridge.
Sento Gosho, Kyoto.

Curved Bridges

Arched bridges have long been associated with Japanese gardens, based on Chinese prototypes where a half circle, reflected in the water, gave the appearance of a full circle or full moon. In Japan the curve is gentler and easier to cross on foot. Curved bridges were, and are, typically made of wood supported on wooden trestles of graded height. All their construction depended on complicated joinery which created strong, stable structures without the benefit of hardware such as nails, screws, nuts or bolts. Curved bridges were particularly advantageous for pond and island gardens and allowed the unhindered passage of pleasure boats. Contrary to Western misconceptions, red, lacquered bridges are rare in Japan, but were a frequent sight in the more flamboyant, early Chinese gardens. Wooden bridges in Japan are usually made of natural, weathered timber, more in keeping with Buddhist beliefs of harmonious existence.

Even in small gardens, a gently curving bridge will establish a Japanese ambience. The choice of style will depend on the formality or informality of the garden. A turf or log bridge will hint at a rustic setting.

CONSTRUCTING CURVED BRIDGES

To create a rustic, curved bridge, a firm base needs to be provided which can be constructed from planks supported by rustic posts and bearers; ideally the posts should stand on stone or concrete plinths. On to the top surface are fastened either logs of equal length or compressed clay topped with turf or moss. Sometimes the materials are combined, leaving a timber surface on which to walk, with moss-covered clay adorning the edges.

Alternatively, a bridge made from precision-cut timbers suggests a more formal, urban setting. To build this type in a domestic setting, the planed cross timbers are fastened to two curved bearers, each of which has been cut from a piece of wood of adequate length to span the water and of adequate depth to accommodate the required curve. The square-cut uprights at each end of the bridge need to be set in concrete to ensure a firm and safe structure. It is usual for a curved plank bridge to have handrails, which may be finished with decorative finials, frequently in the shape of a lotus bud. In the West it is possible to purchase bridges of this style, either ready-made in specified sizes, sometimes from a local garden centre or water garden centre, or larger structures may be custom-made by a reputable manufacturer.

Stepped Bridges

In deference to the belief that evil spirits cross water only in a straight line, bridges are often 'stepped'. For more substantial structures this may mean a zigzag being built into the span. Where the crossing is over a reed bed or swampy area, a

RIGHT: *Construction of bridge.*

BELOW: *Formal curved bridge.*
Kenrokuen garden, Kanazawa.

Yatsuhashi. *Koraku-en garden, Okayama.*

narrow plank bridge of several sections is a recognizable feature. The *yatsuhashi* bridge typically has eight sections which zigzag across the water, just above the surface, supported by a simple system of vertical and horizontal timbers.

Stone Bridges

During the late Kamakura period in the fourteenth century, the use of natural stone for bridges became popular, being incorporated variously into waterfall, stream and pond compositions. The oldest known bridge surviving from this time is made from roughly hewn, flat stones, supported by stone monoliths and positioned at the foot of a large waterfall in the garden of the Tenryu-ji Temple, in the Irashiyama district of Kyoto. The placing of a bridge at the base of a waterfall is still practised. When crossing the bridge, it is possible to have a closer view of the waterfall, and in some cases the bridge is staggered, causing a change of pace and a reawakening of consciousness of the surroundings.

Stone bridges may be either of natural quarried stone or cut to more formal shapes, including gentle arches which perpetuate the structure of earlier wooden bridges. In the West suitably sized pieces of natural granite or slate may be available from stone merchants or garden centres. It is also possible to purchase cut stone bridges, either flat or curved from specialist importers. Some larger merchants offer a custom-made service, where granite is cut to specified sizes.

Increasingly, Japanese-style granite artefacts are being produced in China, where materials are plentiful and labour relatively cheap. The logistics of moving an unwieldy object which may weigh several tons need to be given careful consideration before embarking on such a project.

INSTALLING STONE BRIDGES

When installing stone bridges of any style it is important to ensure that they are balanced and levelled to enable safe negotiation by pedestrians, and that they are firmly secured at each end, preferably by being set in mortar. In keeping with the belief that evil spirits travel in straight lines, a traditional device for breaking the flow of energies over a single-span bridge is to incorporate supporting or guardian stones at the four corners of the bridge – *hashi-ishigumi*. It is customary to use naturally shaped stones of matching geological structure but of different size. One or more stones are set vertically at each corner, ensuring that a visual balance is achieved. The base of each stone should be buried beneath the finished ground level and firmly set in concrete; this is especially important where the stones are actually providing support for the bridge span.

Stone bridges of this type are a strong feature of many *kare-sansui* gardens. As the building of dry gardens associated with Zen Buddhist temples developed during the Muromachi period, the use of stone bridges emphasized the illusion of water and some powerful dry garden landscapes were created. The inclusion of a stone bridge in a domestic Japanese-style garden can bring cohesion to the design, the negotiation of which can evoke the sensation of crossing similar bridges in Japan.

Stepping Stones across Water

In Japanese gardens stepping stones are frequently used to cross water, whether it be a small stream, a large pond or a *kare-sansui* garden. For safety's sake, the stepping stones for crossing water – *sawatari-ishi* – most usually have a larger surface area than those installed in the ground and are placed closer together. Traditionally, natural stones with flattish upper surfaces have been used for crossing water, however, there are some notable exceptions. In the garden of Isui-en in Nara recycled millstones cross the stream to a central island. Similarly, stone blocks reclaimed from a earlier building cross the pond in the Heian shrine garden in Kyoto and these are one of the most recognizable elements of any garden in Japan. *Sawatari-ishi* also bring visitors closer to the water surface, which not only increases the spiritual association with a natural element but improves the appreciation of any koi gliding through the water and foraging around the submerged bottoms of the stones.

Sawatari-ishi *and* tobi-ishi.
Koraku-en garden, Okayama.

Installing Stepping Stones

When installing stepping stones which cross water or *kare-sansui* gardens, their height above water or gravel should be relatively even to reduce the risk of tripping and, as described in Chapter 3, they should be laid in a meandering formation. If it is not possible to obtain stones which are thick enough, it will be necessary to provide a firm base of brick or stone, ideally, with the bottom of the decorative stepping stones below the surface of the water or gravel. In some instances it may be preferable to choose this method since handling the bulk of large stones poses its own problems. Whichever method is used, it is important that all stonework should be firmly set in mortar.

Viewing Platforms

In addition to viewing passing koi from bridges and stepping stones, platforms are provided at the water's edge in gardens of all sizes. These are most usually of natural stone and may be positioned along the route of a path or off to

Koi *viewing platform.*
Jonangu-ji Temple garden, Kyoto.

the side, reached by a subsidiary path. Typically, the stones will be laid randomly and slightly overhang the water so that visitors can safely stand on the stone while encouraging the koi by throwing fish food into the water and enjoying the resulting mêlée and flashes of scaly red, white, gold and silver.

Installing Viewing Platforms

When installing a stone platform it will be necessary to provide a stable base for the stones, especially at the edge of the pond, where a supporting stone or brick structure will be required for the overhanging stones. Preferably, the stone should be of one geological type, in irregular shapes and sizes and laid randomly on a concrete base and set in mortar. As with other areas of natural stone, if the thickness is not uniform, adjustments will need to be made to achieve a level surface. Gaps between stones should be pointed, preferably with a toning mortar.

Pergolas

Pergolas are often constructed above viewing platforms to support sprawling *Wisteria floribunda*. In late April/early May, a profusion of white, mauve or pink racemes cascades over the structure.

Constructing Bamboo Pergolas

In Japan, pergolas are generally constructed from lengths of cut bamboo, approximately 100mm (4in) in diameter. Uprights need to be of adequate length so that pedestrians may pass comfortably underneath, remembering the additional clearance which is necessary when the wisteria is in flower, which may be anything up to 450mm (18in). Horizontal pieces are cut precisely to length and accurately laid at intervals along and across the top of the uprights, all secured with strong, flexible wires and finished with characteristically knotted black hemp.

Tree Supports

Frameworks made from bamboo are frequently used to support the spreading branches of flowering cherry trees. Fan-shaped, trellis-like structures are, in turn, supported on vertical poles at varying levels throughout the tree canopy. The time-consuming process of installing them not only reduces the risk of mechanical breakages to the laden branches but enables visitors to view the blossoms at close quarters.

Some very heavy branch structures are supported by elaborate frameworks of bamboo meticulously constructed in the customary Japanese manner. In a *kare-sansui* garden within the *Kinkaku-ji* Temple complex on the outskirts of Kyoto is an ancient conifer trained over centuries to represent a merchant ship at sea, the 'stern' of which is supported in this way.

Detail of newly constructed bamboo pergola. Daitoku-ji Temple complex, Kyoto.

Bamboo support for weeping sakura. Heian Shrine garden, Kyoto.

ABOVE: Support for mature momiji. Jonangu-ji Temple garden, Kyoto.

RIGHT: Pinus pentaphylla, trained and supported to represent a merchant ship at sea. Kinkaku-ji Temple, Kyoto.

Ancient, deciduous trees may also need to be supported so that gnarled trunks and branches are protected from breakage under their own weight, especially when in full leaf. Revered *Ginkgo biloba* trees which have survived for centuries in shrine and temple forecourts are provided with a system of distinctive cedarwood 'crutches' to distribute the weight of the spreading branches. Similarly, those maples originally planted at an angle to signify a windy, hillside habitat may, with time, threaten to become unbalanced and are also supported by such crutches. Protection from damage by abrasion is provided by wrapping the trunk or branches with pliant hessian or some other natural material. The technique of supporting and protecting 'pines' from snow damage (*yukitsuri*) was described in Chapter 5.

8

Planning a Japanese-Style Garden in the West

From a design point of view and in common with the planning of any other style of garden, there are several considerations to be taken into account when embarking on the creation of a Japanese-style garden.

Choosing the Site

In the first instance, the size and the location of the site and its relationship to any buildings need to be studied. Remember that the layout of traditional Japanese buildings, whether they are shrines, temples, restaurants or houses, more readily facilitates the enjoyment of the garden from inside the building by the use of shutters and screens which open up the sides of buildings, revealing the gardens beyond. Western architecture and the positioning of buildings within their plot does not always make this possible. Within a Western setting consideration has to be given to the optimal siting of a Japanese-style garden; if it is to be adjacent to a building it is necessary to consider whether a mix of Eastern and Western styles is acceptable or whether any steps can be taken to alter the appearance of existing buildings to more closely resemble Japanese architecture.

It may be preferable to dedicate a part of the garden to a Japanese style, where it can be isolated from all Western influences by using bamboo or other screening. Alternatively, the Japanese-style garden may be an integral part of a larger scheme, such as within a garden consisting of several styles from different cultures.

Thought also needs to be given to whether the garden will be discrete within the site or whether there is a distant view which would enhance the garden and could be considered in the design. The practice of using 'borrowed views' (*shakkei*) expands the overall design of many gardens, especially those located in foothills or valleys. When using this technique, the aura of the view is important. In Japan *shakkei* usually include distant hills clad with pines, maples and giant bamboos, sometimes shrouded in mist and sometimes highlighted by sunlight which is particularly striking in spring and autumn. These are unlikely to be found in the West, but gentle, tree-clad hills, valleys and other features can be treasures to complement any garden.

OPPOSITE PAGE:
Installing granite bridge and guardian stones.
Private garden, Dorset, England.

Topography

It is important to be aware of the topography of the site. Is it flat, sloping or undulating, or partly flat and partly sloping? Are the contours suitable for creating a Japanese-style garden, or would it be necessary to undertake regrading? If the latter, is there access for the required machinery, and would potentially substantial earth-moving have any effect on the run-off of water, particularly towards any buildings, or would there be any risk of subsidence? Is the site suitable for building a waterfall, with a possible associated stream

and pond, or is it level enough to create a raked *kare-sansui* garden? The easiest option is to design the garden to fit the topography; however, Japanese designers, ancient and modern, have rarely taken the easiest option, and the manipulation of landscapes to suit the wished-for layout is undergoing a revival in the West.

The topography of the site can influence the choice of materials and the style of the garden. On a steeply sloping site, the viability of manoeuvring large pieces of stone or mature plants is a primary consideration. It may not be possible to enter the site with the necessary lifting equipment,

Manoeuvring a stone bridge with a tripod. Private garden, Hampshire, England.

BELOW: *Moving mature cloud-pruned* Podocarpus. *Tree nursery, Kyoto.*

although considerable weights can be moved short distances by using a tripod system. In such circumstances, the selection of materials will largely depend on the available manpower. Access to the site needs to be viewed in similar terms: if there is only limited access for delivery vehicles, can materials be readily off-loaded and transferred to the site? If the only access is by a narrow gateway or passage, will it allow any equipment to go through? Is that equipment limited to a wheelbarrow, or is there sufficient space for a small digger? In some instances, where access is very restricted, an articulated crane may be used to lift materials over the top of buildings. However, this needs careful management and depends on the budget available for the job. The orientation and the aspect of the proposed garden also need to be taken into consideration, especially when choosing plantings, some of which prefer shade, others may prefer full sun and some are tolerant of both. There may be microclimatic factors to be addressed, such as drying winds which funnel through narrow gaps, or where eddies are created on the leeward side of a hedge or wall. Damaging frost pockets can occur at the lower end of a slope which has a barrier at the bottom, such as a hedge or a building which blocks the passage of descending cold air.

In contrast, a south-facing site, particularly one that is enclosed, may become excessively hot and potentially damaging to plantings. A windy vortex exacerbates the problem. Under such circumstances some protection can be achieved by reducing the drying effect with a lightweight, overhead shading of slatted bamboo or some other material which reduces the effects of sun and wind but allow reduced light to filter through and any rainfall to permeate. It would also be advisable to install an automatic irrigation system which is activated when the relative humidity drops below a recommended level. However, before this can be undertaken, the local regulations on the use of water would have to be checked.

Soil Type

Another deciding factor in the choice of plantings for a Japanese-style garden is the soil type. Japan is mostly granite and other hard bedrock stone yielding a soil in which acid-loving plants flourish. In Europe, by contrast, there is significant variation in local stone and soil types, which can influence the choice of plants and other materials. Where the soil pH is higher than 7.0 (neutral) the usual practice is to choose plants which will tolerate the lime content. It may be possible to create some areas which are more acidic; ideally, these need to be isolated from the native soil, either in sunken containers or raised beds, bearing in mind that the ground water will always remain alkaline. In these conditions it is advisable to apply sequestered iron in spring and autumn; this can be purchased in granular form ready to be dissolved, diluted and watered around the plants.

In addition to ascertaining the soil pH, a fundamental consideration is the structure of the soil. One with a high sand and gravel content will drain rapidly and any nutrients will be leached out. The addition of large quantities of well-rotted organic material will improve the structure and its water-holding capacity, as well as enabling any plantings to form stronger root structures. However, it will be essential to replenish organic material regularly. The installation of an irrigation system will also ensure that water can be supplied during any prolonged periods of dry weather. Where irrigation is provided, the incorporation of a soluble fertilizer during the growing season will be beneficial.

Conversely, soils with a high clay content are usually rich in nutrients and retain a high percentage of water, but are equally detrimental to optimal plant growth. Following periods of high rainfall, clayey soils become so saturated that anaerobic conditions can result which will deprive plant root systems of necessary oxygen and nutrients.

Following long periods of dry weather, clayey soils will become dry and hard, also depriving roots of oxygen, with the additional complications of also reducing the available water and increasing the temperature of the soil top layer. The addition of gypsum (hydrated calcium sulphate) can improve the soil structure to some extent; however, the inclusion of well-rotted organic material before planting allows increased aeration, improved drainage and a healthier medium in which to grow plants. As in sandy soils, organic matter will be broken down rapidly by the natural activities of soil life. Again, to ensure the continued improvement in structure and plant health, organic material should be replenished regularly, preferably in early spring and again in autumn.

Choosing Materials

Plants

Having taken these factors into account, the choice of plantings can begin. To make the process easier, it is advisable to contact specialist growers as well as those importers who are most likely to have specimen plants, including those pruned and trained into traditional Japanese shapes. When gardens are built in Japan, the aim is to create a scene which appears to have existed for many years; fully mature trees achieve that illusion and, where the budget allows, mature specimens create the instant, mature garden.

'Hard' Materials

The availability of hard materials is also a deciding factor in choosing the design of any Japanese-style garden. It is important to have an up-to-date knowledge of stocks of items such as bamboo screens, carved stone artefacts and natural stone materials, whether they are gravel, water-washed boulders or large stones for constructing waterfalls and bridges, for instance. Items available one year may not be not be in stock in another. Imported items vary from season to season, and regulations on quarrying or the removal of natural stone are continually changing. There are suppliers who claim that their products are 'authentic Japanese style', but it is wise to check that this claim is valid. For instance, bamboo fences and screens should be of recognizable Japanese styling and so avoid any which are more typically Chinese or Indonesian. Similarly with granite artefacts, claims are often made that coloured water basins and lanterns are appropriate for a Japanese-style garden. Far from the truth, grey granite is the intrinsic material of Japan, not green, red or pink. Pre-cast

Stored 'hard' materials.
Landscape gardening company, Kyoto.

concrete products, glazed in bright colours would never be seen.

The Style of Garden

Having chosen the site for a Japanese garden and pondered on the above points, the choice of style may now be considered. Is it desirable to produce a garden representative of any particular era? Do non-Shintoists and Buddhists want the heavily symbolic aspects of those beliefs in their gardens? Or is it preferable to follow one's instincts and personal requirements to create a place of peace and tranquillity, incorporating a mixture of Japanese styles? Western gardens have also followed fashions and economic circumstances. Historically, the magnificently designed gardens of Europe and elsewhere were mostly the domain of royalty, the aristocracy, wealthy landowners, bankers and the like. The poorer sections of society, if indeed they were fortunate enough to have access to any land, were more likely to use it for food

production, raising livestock and growing vegetables and fruit, with herbs for medicinal purposes, and sometimes with an area of ornamental, cottage-style plantings.

Recreational and Practical Considerations

With socio-economic changes and influences from cultures such as North America and Australia, domestic land use has also changed. More often gardens are used as extensions to the house, creating another living space and encompassing several recreational and practical activities. A variety of games may be played which need to be accommodated within the space available – perhaps a swimming pool, a sandpit for the children, places to sit and enjoy the sun or to shelter from it, places to enjoy meals in the open air – a barbecue, perhaps – an area for storing logs and coal, another for compost, a place to hang the laundry, access for vehicles, parking for caravans and so on.

Traditionally, the Japanese lifestyle has been in great contrast to the Western, and Japanese gardens do not make allowances for most of the recreational activities which have developed elsewhere. When creating a Japanese-style garden, is it possible or desirable to separate the garden from Western requirements? Or can provision be made for those activities considered most important to the lifestyle of the household? It is probably preferable to separate those activities most alien to the Japanese concepts of simplicity, peace and tranquillity, such as the presence of rubbish bins, storage sheds and car maintenance areas.

The provision of outside seating and dining spaces has become an integral part of much Western life. Some restaurants in Japan take advantage of their garden settings and have outside eating areas, but this is uncommon in domestic settings. However, the thoughtful use of materials can usually achieve an acceptable compromise.

Ball games, so popular in the West, are not part of Japanese garden culture. However, during the Heian period a type of football was enjoyed by players who formed a ring, and aimed to keep the ball in the air by skilful footwork – no chasing up and down nor protecting goalmouths by falling on muddy surfaces. In keeping with so many Japanese art forms, the game was gently elegant and the participants dressed in the traditional, colourful costumes of the day.

There may be other recreational reasons which lead enthusiasts in the West to consider a Japanese style of garden. Perhaps to create an appropriate setting for their treasured koi carp or to display to advantage a collection of bonsai. In either case, the provision of a suitable pond for the koi or a separate benched area for the bonsai will need to be included in the total design.

Maintenance Considerations

Factors sometimes overlooked when planning any garden are the necessary on-going care and the individual circumstances of the owner. Such considerations include: will there be skilled labour available to manage the plantings? Is there sufficient knowledge to maintain any flowing water and the associated pumps, filters and electrical equipment? If koi are to be kept, can they be maintained in good health? In dry weather can irrigation be supplied? Ideally, in order to enjoy any garden the essential maintenance should be well within the physical and financial capabilities of its owner – and a special quality of a good designer is to take all these factors into account.

ABOVE: Enjoying a Buddhist meal. Daitoku-ji complex, Kyoto.

RIGHT: Heian-style football game. Nishi-hongan-ji Temple, Kyoto.

9

Maintenance

The detailed maintenance programme for a Japanese-style garden is as important as the concept, the design and the construction. Some techniques are practised universally in the upkeep of plantings, hard materials and buildings. However, a significant contribution to the successful interpretation of any Japanese-style garden depends on the recognition of the significance of all the component elements within it and of their unique relationship to each other. A prerequisite to creating such a garden is the acceptance that it will not take care of itself, and that time and money will need to be invested in maintaining the ethos of the garden.

The aspect of these gardens which is the least familiar to gardeners outside Japan is the skilful training and pruning of trees and shrubs which is essential in developing and sustaining their characteristic shapes.

ABOVE:
Autumnal needle removal.
Private garden, Kyoto.

OPPOSITE PAGE:
Needle-grooming Pinus thunbergii.
Private garden, Kyoto.

Conifers

Needle Removal

Some of the hallmarks of an authentic Japanese garden are the 'pine' trees which have been trained into stylized shapes over many years. To maintain their clean profiles requires the regular removal of old needles and other debris, as well as the thinning of new needles produced during the year. Late autumn is the optimal season to undertake this time-consuming and labour-intensive activity.

Beginning at the top of the tree, and armed only with secateurs and gloves to protect the hands from prickly and sticky needles, one or several gardeners work downwards through every branch. The cleaning process (*soji*) consists of the removing of all unwanted debris, including dead leaves and litter from other trees, cutting out any dead branches which have been revealed during the year and removing dead and fading needles from the tree. Unlike deciduous trees which shed their leaves every autumn, 'pines' retain their needles for several years, and these include those which are no longer actively photosynthesizing and have become brown and dry. Their removal results, not only in a cleaner, fresher appearance of the tree, but in the freer movement of air and access of light for the newer needles, encouraging healthier growth.

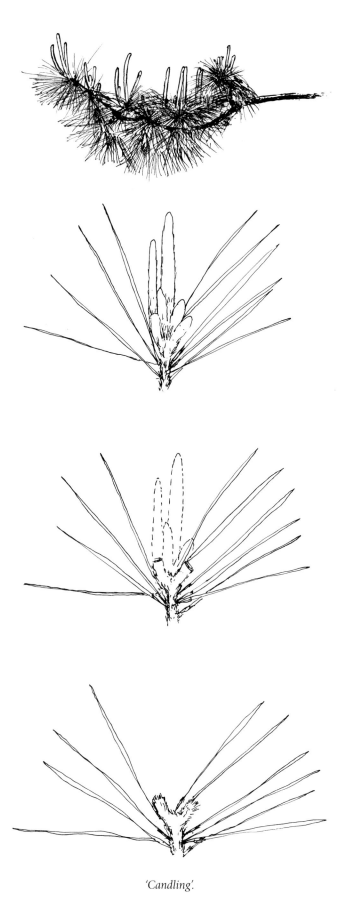

'Candling'.

Needle Grooming

'Needle grooming' can be done at the same time as the cleaning process. This technique leads to the characteristic appearance of spreading 'pines' so familiarly depicted in ancient Chinese ink drawings as well as on Japanese artefacts.

The only tools required for this procedure are skilled hands: while holding the branches with one hand, the downward-pointing needles growing on the underside of the branch are removed with the other. Those which point sideways or upwards are left intact. Where it is desirable to alter the shape of a particular branch, either by elongation or by filling out a specific area, downward-pointing needles are preserved since they will continue to grow and build the required framework.

Candle Removal

The removal of the emerging shoots or 'candles' encourages dense, bushy growth by redirecting energy into other parts of the tree. To achieve this lush appearance, new shoots are either pinched back or removed by hand in late spring. 'Candling' most usually maintains an existing tree shape, while improving its mass. However, where looser growth or longer branches are the aim, selective candle removal should be tackled with care.

Creating Cascading Branches

Where the objective is to create the appearance of an ancient, windswept pine tree, clinging to a craggy cliff, it is particularly important not to remove the candles at the tips of those branches which will cascade downwards. To achieve a cascade, choose a branch which is on the outside of a curve. Each year remove the top growth above an imagined line, while allowing the tip of the selected branch to grow outwards. Gradually, the carefully managed branch will become elongated, giving the tree that windswept look.

In natural habitats, trees cascade over water in their search for light. Where a river bank has been eroded over time or where competing trees push the tree nearer to the water's edge, the cascading growth is emphasized. In Japanese gardens trees cascading beside water are another illusionary trick. Branches overhanging the water are encouraged to grow by retaining their leading shoots, at the same time foreshortening the branches on the land side and maintaining a reduced total height and balanced tree shape.

Autumnal cleaning and needling will ensure the health and strength of the tree, but for waterside specimens this may involve having to venture into the water to work on the overhanging branches.

Maintaining a tree shape.
Ritsurin Koen, Takamatsu.

Pruned willow.
Higashi Geisha District, Kanazawa.

Deciduous Trees

Pruning Naturally Weeping Trees

When pruning such trees, the primary objectives are to create a serpentine trunk and to open up the front of the tree to emphasize those branches which are growing on the outward curves of the trunk. The aim is to produce short branches which grow upwards and outwards, with plumes of feathery growth cascading downwards. Smaller branches which are growing downwards are removed. The technique is most commonly used on smaller weeping trees, such as willows, *Salix babylonica*, which have been restricted in size, as well as birches, *Betula pendula*, which particularly lend themselves to this treatment. The open, cascading growth reveals the tree

bark and is especially striking after heavy rain when the colours and texture of the bark are emphasized.

Maintaining 'Layered' Growth

Unlike Western gardens, where an abundance of foliage is treasured, in Japan the thinning out of new growth is practised, creating lighter, more delicate trees, with layered branches which catch the light and nod gracefully in the breeze. This is particularly suitable for the colourful maples (*momiji*) and gingkos (*icho*) which enhance many Japanese gardens and street scenes.

Branches are selected which are appropriately spaced around the trunk, either forming a uniform shape or, especially in the case of *momiji*, the much-favoured, overhanging

Layered momiji.
Near Saiho-ji temple, Kyoto.

style. Unwanted branches are removed close to the main trunk during late summer or early autumn, and the new, dividing growth at the branch tips is either removed totally or the growth on the top side of the branches is allowed to remain while the new growth on their undersides is removed. The goal is to retain the uppermost foliage in a well-balanced and aesthetically pleasing arrangement, at the same time cleanly removing any growth which has developed along the underside of the branches. This technique ensures that foliage nearer to the trunk continues to flourish with its exposure to good light levels, as well as the availability of nutrients which would otherwise be directed into any new growth.

avoids the syndrome of bare, light-deprived branches carrying an overload of foliage at their extremities.

In some circumstances, shearing may be the only option. For instance, in late spring/early summer, when there are so many demands on time, in order to maintain a neat and tidy Japanese-style garden the quickest method will need to be employed. At such a time a total light pruning with hand shears will yield a compact appearance, and also allow rhododendrons to set buds for the following year's flowering. In late summer/early autumn when the demands on time are fewer, hand pruning with secateurs or snippers can be resumed. This will clean up the interior of the plants and thin out the dense, peripheral growth which will have developed through the growing season.

Shrubs

Maintaining Rounded Shapes

The maintaining of shrubs in rounded or other formalized shapes is achieved in two ways. The most accurate method requires the use of manually-operated secateurs or snippers, which results in optimal plant growth and health. In late spring/early summer peripheral growth is considered case by case. With *Rhododendron* spp. (azalea) and *Buxus microphylla*, all soft, new growth is removed, as well as some older growth deeper into the plants; this assures a more robust plant with vigorous new growth being formed from the interior, which

O-Karikomi

Similar techniques will be applied where trees and shrubs are clipped to a prescribed shape to depict scenery (*o-karikomi*) such as mountains, islands in the sea or waves in the ocean.

Wisteria

To ensure the tight growth and optimal flowering of *Wisteria* spp. diligent pruning is necessary. In the first winter, lateral growth should be cut back by one-third and sublaterals to two or three buds. Once the plant is established, all

Shearing Rhododendron.
Private garden, Kyoto.

BELOW: *Pruned* Wisteria *in bud.*
Private garden, Hampshire, England.

and shrubs which gain in girth as well as height throughout their lifetime. Bamboos are grasses which put on a fast burst of growth once a year. The ultimate width and height of each culm is contained in the emerging shoot, the above ground development being solely related to the lengthening of internodes and the unfolding of foliage.

Large Bamboos

To control the spread of tall-growing bamboos, remove new shoots from places where they are not wanted, either by breaking them off by hand or by cutting them with a sharp knife or secateurs just below ground level. Where it is feasible, another limiting technique, carried out in the autumn, is to cut through the edge of the bamboo grove with a long, flat spade, which severs the rhizomes and reduces the growth potential for the following season. In Japan, shoots are thinned out from the base so that each culm may be appreciated. Older shoots are removed, together with all leaf litter and other debris, revealing the colour and vigour of the younger, superior culms.

Where bamboo is used as a screen or hedge, this process has a twofold benefit. If a stand of bamboo matures unchecked, a thicket of culms will result, bearing the bulk of the foliage at the top of the shoots, with little lower down, thus reducing the effectiveness of the planting as a screen. By removing older culms which have lost their beauty, new growth is encouraged and, depending on the species of bamboo, foliage will be borne along the length of the new shoots.

shoots not needed to form the desired framework should be removed in late summer and midwinter. Spurs should be reduced to leave two or three buds on which flower buds will be set for the following spring.

Bamboo

To successfully maintain bamboos of any genera, it is useful to realize that their growth habit is unlike that of trees

Bamboos of Mid Height

Many of the bamboo species which are shorter growing, attaining a height of 1 to 2m (3–6½ft), tend to form invasive, spreading rhizomatous systems, which become more vigorous each year as the area of foliage increases. Some of these species are tolerant of heavy shade, such as *Sasa veitchii*, which forms the natural forest floor vegetation in Japan and is useful as an underplanting in larger Japanese-style gardens in a wide range of climatic zones.

Sasa, *Sasaella* and *Pleioblastus* spp. all have vigorous underground growth, so it is wise to choose a site where it can grow unchecked, otherwise their spreading into other parts of the garden will need to be curbed. Where the removal of emerging shoots will be routine it is important to ensure that, in so doing, other plantings will not be damaged. An alternative is to provide an impenetrable barrier,

*Thinned-out bamboo grove.
Keihanna koen, near Kyoto.*

either of concrete or heavy duty plastic, both of which should be buried to a depth of 1m (3ft). A specimen may be planted in a large pot placed below soil level, but this is not feasible where ground covering is required and vigilant attention to watering will be needed.

Ground-Covering Bamboos

Some bamboos are suitable for planting as low-growing ground cover and are often used for the green sward which, in the West, would most likely be the more familiar lawn grasses. *Pleioblastus pygmaeus*, *P. pumilis* and *Sasaella ramosa* are ideal bamboos for ground cover since they are amenable both to occasional mowing with a high-set mower blade, to strimming or to hand shearing with long-bladed, sharp shears.

To maintain bamboos in good heart, mulching with organic material both retains soil moisture and replenishes the organic matter in the soil. The dry and unwanted foliage from the bamboo plants can be useful for this purpose. The application of a high-nitrogen lawn fertilizer in spring and late summer will also encourage healthy growth. In drought conditions such fertilizers should be applied only in a soluble liquid form, as it is advisable to dilute a granular feed. Failing that, you could simply wait for some steady rain!

Other Ground-Covering Plants

The maintenance of other ground-covering plants, such as mosses, *Ophiopogon* 'tamaryu', *Soleirolia soleirolii* and lawns, will also be a continuing task.

Mosses

Where it is possible to achieve the healthy growth of mosses as ground cover some maintenance will be necessary. Any fallen leaves and twigs will need to be raked or brushed away and dead or dying patches of moss removed. In the gardens of Japan the maintenance of the hallowed moss is considered as an honour, with teams of gardeners quietly working their way through it, removing any unwanted 'weeds', including grass, and depositing debris into baskets woven from bamboo leaves. To indicate that gardens are cared for in this way, bamboo rakes, brushwood brooms and the characteristic baskets are displayed in a corner of the garden or near a building.

*Removing grass from moss.
Ginkaku-ji Temple, Kyoto.*

Ophiopogon japonicus *(tamaryu)*

Although *tamaryu* is a good-natured ground cover, suitable for use where the conditions are not suitable for moss to proliferate, as in hot, dry climates or on exposed sites, some maintenance will be required. Until it is established, it will be necessary to remove any weeds which emerge between the young plants, as well as removing all fallen leaves, flowers and twigs. It is also advisable to deter predators such as slugs and snails since plants which have been nibbled lose their vigour as well as becoming less attractive and effective as ground cover. Top dress in the autumn with a well-rotted leaf mould. The application of a soluble, high-nitrogen fertilizer in the spring will encourage new growth.

Soleirolia soleirolii

Until it is established, the maintenance of *Soleirolia soleirolii* involves the removal of any weed growth and plant debris. But once established and forming a ground-hugging mat, it may spread into areas where it is not required; it can be removed by hand thinning. In shaded areas, lusher, taller growth may result which can be reduced with a good quality strimmer or by hand-shearing. In colder areas there may be frost damage, causing blackening of the leafy growth; this can be removed either by hand or by gentle raking. Recovery will be rapid with new growth in the spring.

Grasses

The cultivation and maintenance of grass as ground cover will depend on the climatic zone and the types of grass which can be grown. As a general rule, regular mowing during the growing season ensures tillering and new growth. Feeding with a high-nitrogen fertilizer will replenish the photosynthetic material which has been removed by mowing. Some proprietary lawn foods also contain moss- and weed-killers; these will need to be chosen according to the species of grass. Weeds can also be removed by hand.

In high temperature areas or where soils are free-draining, automatic irrigation is advisable. However, its installation will depend on the budget and local water-authority regulations. Top dressing with finely-milled, composted, organic materials will also supply nutrients and at the same time improve the soil structure and moisture retention.

Water

The maintenance of any major water installations such as waterfalls, steams or ponds, together with their associated plantings, is vital to their continued success.

Spring

Installations will need to be checked for winter damage and leaks. If repairs are necessary, the pond, stream or waterfall will need to be drained to a level where access to the damage is possible. If the bottom of the installation is damaged and the whole needs to be drained, a temporary home for fish and other pond life will have to be provided in a holding tank, which should be filled with water from the pond. This provides a good opportunity on which to check the health of all the creatures.

Those bog and aquatic plants which have become matted or reduced in vigour will need to be lifted, divided and replanted; any new plants may also be introduced.

All electrical equipment will need to be cleaned and checked for efficient functioning and safety. For large installations it may be advisable to employ a specialist company.

Summer

The planting of new aquatics continues through early to mid-summer to ensure their establishment during the growing season. At the same time, remove all plant and other debris from the water. Treatment for algae may become necessary during periods of prolonged sunlight and high temperature. Check which additives are safe for fish and other pond life, and which are acceptable to the relevant water authority.

The regular cleaning of pumps and filters should continue. It is vital to maintain water levels to cover all the associated equipment, as well as plastic or butyl liners which will deteriorate if exposed to ultraviolet light. Evaporation will be highest during the summer, particularly where there are waterfalls or any other sources of moving water. If a hosepipe is used for topping up, be aware of any hosepipe bans.

Autumn

As aquatic and bog plants die back, remove all foliage and cut stems to below the surface of the water. Leave floating plants which depend on over-wintering material to provide new growth for the following year. Any tender aquatics in containers should be removed and given protection for the winter. Established plantings such as *Iris laevigata* may be lifted, divided and replanted. At the same time, the soil can be dug over and improved by the addition of organic material and/or horticultural sand where this is required.

Unless pumps are to be used throughout the winter, they can be removed from the water in late autumn, drained, cleaned and oiled.

Winter

Winter is the time of the least maintenance activity, other than to continue removing any plant litter from the water. It is, however, advisable to protect static water from freezing since this may cause damage to liners. This may be done by floating either logs or bundles of straw on the surface of the water; these will take the impact of any expansion due to freezing. In areas with excessively cold winters or where fish are over-wintered in the pond, it may be preferable to use a low-voltage electrical heater for the purpose.

Tsukubai *and* Shishi-Odoshi

Pumps and filters associated with *tsukubai* and *shishi-odoshi* will also need regular checking and cleaning. Where there is an isolated sump for circulating the water, it is particularly important to ensure that water levels are maintained to cover submersible pumps. Any associated, decorative pebbles should be removed and cleaned of soil and other unwanted matter. Where there is a grid this too should be cleaned and any blockages removed. At the same time, clean the interior of the sump and the water basin. All associated pipework needs to be checked for breakages and leaks. Bamboo spouts and ladles which have deteriorated need to be replaced.

In areas with very low winter temperatures it may be advisable to drain *tsukubai* and *shishi-odoshi* installations. Pumps and filters may then be removed, checked, cleaned, oiled and stored for the winter.

Gravels

In *kare-sansui* gardens, maintenance continues throughout the year. All intrusive debris should be removed whenever necessary which, in autumn, will probably be a daily, early-morning routine. As *kare-sansui* gardens are usually forbidden

Cleaning debris from tsukubai *stones.*
Jonangu-ji temple, Kyoto.

Replacing bamboo kakei *and ladle support.*
Private garden, Kyoto.

to pedestrians, footprints in the gravel or sand are unacceptable. Consequently, following every excursion into the area all evidence of human activity needs to be removed by raking the aggregate, either into a pristine, flat surface or into characteristic 'wave' patterns.

On occasion, it may be necessary to replenish the aggregates which have become depleted. However, as any existing materials will have inevitably changed colour through weathering or colonization by rudimentary plants such as lichen and mosses, it is important to ensure the uniformity of the end result, either by mixing the existing materials with the new or by providing a covering over the whole area to a uniform depth. Ideally, any topping up materials should be obtained from the same source as the original material.

Removing debris from pathway.
Chikurin-in, Otsu.

Paving and Stepping Stones

In addition to the aesthetic qualities of paving and stepping stones, it is of paramount importance to ensure the safety of pedestrians. Check that all fixing and pointing materials are intact and that stepping stones are stable. Where there is any deterioration in the mortar, remove all loose material and replace with a compatible mix. If the surface is liable to become slippery, it will be necessary to remove any plant material, such as algae or fallen leaves, either by hand brushing or with a power-assisted hose. There are anti-slip preparations available which are applied with a brush and will also need regular renewal.

Timber and Cut Bamboo

Timber

Any timber in a garden, whether it is a verandah, a bridge or any other structure, will need regular maintenance. Any rotting or damaged timbers will have to be replaced and the whole structure treated with a non-toxic preservative. The timber most widely used in Japan is *Cryptomeria japonica*, which has a relatively trouble-free and long life. When choosing a preservative for any timber, it is preferable to endeavour to replicate the native colouring of seasoned wood.

Cut Bamboo

Being a natural material, cut bamboo has a useful lifespan of about five years. With exposure to drying sun, wind, as well as rain and frost, bamboo becomes brittle and weakens and fungal growth may occur, accelerating the breaking-down of the canes. The application of yacht varnish which has been diluted with white spirit will lengthen the life of cut bamboo, but there is an inevitability about the need for replacement. In Japan the uniformity of bamboo fences, screens and plant supports is an important aspect of their visual impact, therefore patching up or the random replacement of canes is unacceptable and the replacement of the whole structure will be necessary.

The regular checking of the black hemp will also be necessary and is particularly important where ties and knots hold the structure together. Hemp may break down more quickly than the bamboo and the preferred practice is to replace it in its entirety. However, modern synthetic materials are more durable and likely to last intact for the life of the bamboo.

The Gardens of Japan

Although the spirituality and philosophy is expressed in the gardens created throughout the Japanese archipelago, it is in the more temperate central regions of Honshu and Shikoku that they abound and are preserved into the present century. A large majority of the gardens are in and around the ancient city of Kyoto, which was the capital of Japan from 794 until 1603, when the seat of power was moved to Edo, a settlement which today we know as Tokyo. This period encompassed a time of prolific garden construction and the development of different styles appropriate to the cultural and spiritual beliefs of the day. Many of the gardens have public access and can be enjoyed throughout the year.

The gardens described and illustrated below are divided into two groups, those in the first spread from Shikoku, through the hinterland of Honshu, including the Japanese Alps and areas in the vicinity of Kyoto; those in the second are the gardens of Kyoto. There is a modest entry fee for most of them, usually in the range of ¥250 to ¥800. Seasonal opening times may be checked with local tourist offices. Photography is permitted in most gardens; however, some temples reserve their right to privacy. In a few there may be bans for particular reasons, such as at Katsura Rikyu, where visitors straying from the stepping stones to obtain the best compositions were trampling on and destroying the precious mosses.

From the descriptions and illustrations of many of the gardens can be gathered more ideas and information to include in designs when creating Japanese-style gardens in West. The greater the authenticity the more likely it will be to achieve an atmosphere suggesting peace, tranquillity and contemplation, the very essence of Japanese gardens throughout the ages.

Japan Other than Kyoto

Takamatsu: Ritsurin Koen

Kagawa Prefecture; Edo period; strolling garden, open throughout the year; the garden of Ritsurin park is situated near the town of Takamatsu, in the Kagawa province on the island of Shikoku, trains run regularly from the main JR station in Okayama on Honshu to Takamatsu, crossing the

OPPOSITE PAGE:
Sawatari-ishi.
*Heian Shrine
Garden.*

RIGHT:
*'Drum'-shaped shrubs
and curved bridge.
Ritsurin Koen.*

*Path descending the hill.
Koraku-en.*

Within the park are also situated the Centre for the Encouragement of Commerce and Industry and the Sanuki Folkcraft Museum, which is open to the public and has a variety of displays of local crafts.

Okayama: Koraku-en

Okayama Prefecture; Edo period; strolling garden, open throughout the year; access to the garden from Okayama JR station, either by local tram or bus.

A strolling garden, the building of which was begun in 1686 and was completed in 1700, covering an area of 13ha (31 acres), it is typical of the Edo period. It was owned by the Ikeda family until 1884, when ownership was transferred to the Okayama Prefecture who opened the garden to the public. In 1871 the garden was renamed Koraku-en after an old Chinese saying, 'First worry, then enjoy'. Koraku-en is recognized as one of Japan's three most beautiful gardens and in 1952 was designated as a special scenic location under Japan's Property Protection Law. The garden is built on a sandbank of the Asahi River and is overlooked on a neighbouring shore by the imposing multistoreyed Okayama Castle, 'The Black Crow Castle' – *Ujo* – views of which are incorporated in the garden (*shakkei*). The flowing river water is used to full effect with streams, ponds and waterfalls. Plantings of interest within the garden include a replica tea plantation and rice field in the traditional 3 × 3 formation. There are groves of cherry trees, plum trees and maples, as well as an iris garden which is crossed by a wooden *Yatsuhashi* bridge, providing interest for every season. The most distinctive features of Korakuen are the naturalistic hill, with a gentle climb via stepping stones, between trimmed azalea hedges, at the top of which there is a resting place from where the garden, the surrounding hills and Misao Mountain can be viewed. There is a stream in which are set large, natural stones, which cuts through the wooden floor of the unusually designed, Ryuten-tei tea house (Tea Shop by the Stream) (*see* p.22).

Takahashi: Raikyuji Temple Garden

Okayama Prefecture; Edo period; *kare-sansui* with plantings; check opening times; from Okayama take the Hakubi Line train to Bitchu Takahashi station, going northwards; Raikyuji Temple and Garden are about a 15min walk away, local maps indicate the exact location; to see the garden it is necessary to enter the temple building and cross to the viewing verandah.

Named in the sixteenth century after the Lord of Matuyama Castle, Yorihisa Raikyu Ueno, this temple and garden of the Rinzai sect of Buddhism was built by Governor Enshu Kobori,

Seto Inland Sea by the multi-span Seto Ohashi bridge, a journey which can be somewhat unpredictable during a hurricane; from Takamatsu there are either local buses, or a single-track train with a station near Ritsurin Koen.

The garden was first built in the seventeenth century as a Daimyo strolling garden with ponds, islands and tea houses. Covering 75ha (180 acres), it is one of the largest in Japan and in 1997 was classified as a 'special beauty spot'. Mount Shiun forms a backdrop to the garden which is divided into two parts, the Southern Garden housing several ponds as well as the Kikugetsu and Higurashi-tei pavilions. The North Garden includes the iris garden in Gunouchi Pond, transversed by staggered plank bridges. The most readily recognizable features of Ritsurin Koen are the long, curved wooden bridges, one of which is particularly steep, the shrubs pruned into drum-shapes, and the gnarled 'pines', which are regularly pruned and 'needled' by numerous gardeners.

'Crane' and 'Turtle' islands.
Raikyu-ji.

Front garden.
The Warrior's House Museum.

an established garden designer, who took refuge in the temple from a war which was raging in Bittyu Province. The garden is in front of the abbot's quarters (*hojo*) and is in the 'Horai' style, which induces spiritual peacefulness and harmony. In the silver sand are a crane island and a turtle island, set beneath the backdrop of Mount Atago. A clipped azalea hedge wends its way along one side of the *kare-sansui*, while an impressive example of *o-karikomi* dominates one end of the garden. This particular grouping of clipped azaleas is believed to represent waves in the ocean. A replication of Enshu's curving path across the *kare-sansui* garden of Konchi-in in Kyoto leads from the *shoin* to other temple buildings, accessible only to the resident monks (*see* p.74).

Takahashi: The Warrior's House Museum

Ishibiya-cho Street, Okayama Prefecture.

A short walk further along the street from Raikyu-ji Temple, passing through Edo-style mud walls, topped with clay tiles or reed thatching, there is a small samurai house and garden open to the public. Entrance is through a traditional Japanese-style gateway. Crossing the threshold, a stepping-stone path traverses the garden to the main entrance of the house, passing a grouping including a snow viewing lantern (*yukimi-gata*), with overhanging, heavily pruned pine tree.

Himeji: Nishi-Oyashiki-Ato Garden, Himeji Koko-en

Open throughout the year; from the JR mainline station of Himeji, going northwards the garden and Castle are a 15min walk or a 7min bus ride to Ote-mon bus stop.

Under the walls of Himeji Castle lie the gardens of Himeji Koko-en, a series of gardens constructed in 1992 to commemorate the 100th anniversary of the establishment of Himeji municipality, coinciding with the designation of

Himeji Castle as a UNESCO World Heritage Site. Nine separate gardens occupy the site of the former Lord's West Residence (*nishi-oyakashi*). The name *koko-en* is derived from the name of a school founded in 1692 in Himeji by its last Lord. The nine gardens encapsulate styles of the Edo period and are surrounded by mud walls typical of the period, each of a different colour, replicating the original walls and signifying the identity of the individual samurai owners. The gardens include a tea ceremony garden and tea rooms, as well as others designed to resemble the countryside, pine forests and bamboo plantations. Unusual features are the *nae-no-niwa*, the garden of seedlings, in which seedlings formerly grown in the Edo period are cultivated in wooden plant beds, bordered by *Camellia chinensis* used to make green tea. Similarly in the *hana-no-niwa* (the garden of flowers) are grown garden flowers of the Edo period and rare wild plants. From the *nagare-no-hiwa-niwa* (flatly landscaped garden) unhindered views of the main keep and the West Bailey of Himeji Castle can be enjoyed. The wooden structure built between the fourteenth and the seventeenth century is one of the best preserved Japanese multi-storeyed fortifications. Painted white and sometimes referred to as the White Heron Castle, Himeji Castle can be seen for miles around, benevolently protecting the local population.

Waterfall and pond viewed from tea house, Koko-en.

BELOW: *Stone grouping, lower garden, Ichijodani.*

Fukui: The Remains of the Asakura Family Residence and Gardens

Fukui Prefecture; Muromachi period; open throughout the year; from Fukui JR mainline station, a local train on the Etsumi North Line takes 20min to Ichijodani station, with

a walk to the site; local buses from Fukui stop close to the main entrance and information offices, Asakurayakata Mae bus stop.

Although now mostly in ruins, there are some powerful remnants of the headquarters of the Asakura clan who ruled the area for 103 years during the time known as the Sengoku period (1471–1573). In a rural valley setting with bamboo-clad hills as a backdrop, the boundary of the main villa is defined by a Chinese-style, shingle-roofed gateway, *Chukoku-mon*, said to be guarded by the spirit of Yoshikage, the last head of the Asakura family. Climbing the hillside, and following a marked route, the four gardens are revealed. Each was built with large granite standing stones, now covered in moss and lichen. The largest garden, which has been restored, includes a waterfall composition with water tumbling into a pond. On one side of the stepped waterfall is a huge rock and on the other an overhanging maple tree, with golden autumn foliage. The grandeur of the stone settings at Ichijo-dani indicates the wealth of the Asakura family. The stones are ideal examples on which to base designs for more modest rock groupings.

Kanazawa: Kenrokuen Garden

Ishikawa Prefecture; Edo period; strolling garden, open throughout the year; from the JR mainline station of Kanazawa local buses regularly pass the main entrance to Kenrokuen Garden.

Kenrokuen is reputed to be one of the three most beautiful gardens in Japan. Situated on a hilltop site, it was originally the outer garden of nearby Kanazawa Castle built between the

ABOVE: Kotoji *lantern.*
Kenrokuen.

LEFT: Karigane bashi.
Kenrokuen.

seventeenth and the nineteenth centuries as a private garden for the Maeda clan. In 1871, at the end of Japan's feudal era, it was opened to the public. The literal meaning of the name *Kenrokuen* is that it combines the six attributes of a perfect garden: spaciousness, seclusion, careful arrangement, antiquity, abundant water and broad views. A strolling garden of about 10ha (24 acres), the garden of Kenrokuen can be enjoyed at any season of the year, with plantings of plum trees (*ume*) heralding the new year, followed in late spring by the flowering of 400 cherries (*sakura*). In early summer the irises bloom in a gently running stream, near to the famous Kotoji, or 'two-legged lantern'. Deciduous trees provide mottled shade throughout the summer and in autumn turn to shades of red and yellow. During winter the meticulous symmetry of *yukitsuri* (snow guard) straw ropes, stand out against the skyline. Within the garden are several large ponds, connected by flowing streams; the water is obtained from the Saigawa River, which is 100m (330ft) above sea level, and a system of channels, completed in 1632, carries the water into the garden. Several bridges traverse the streams, the most distinctive of which is the *Karigane bashi* ('Flying Geese') Bridge, which is a combination of eleven tortoise-shaped stones set in a 'V' shape to represent geese flying in formation. A thatched tea house of typical rustic design overlooks the *Midori-taki* (Green Waterfall), which flows into the gourd-shaped lake nearby (*see* p.133).

Kanazawa: Seison-Kaku Mansion Garden

Open most of the year, but closed on Wednesdays and between 29 December and 2 January annually.

Within the grounds of Kenrokuen is a shingle-roofed mansion built in 1863 by Maeda Nariyasu for his mother to live in in comfortable retirement. The mansion of Seison-saku is considered to be a building of great elegance, designated as an 'Important Cultural Property' and housing a museum of samurai artefacts. The gardens may be enjoyed from within the building. The *Tsukushi* (horsetail) Garden is on a level site, with a careful arrangement of trees and flowing streams. The *omoto* garden contains several miniature hills and old trees.

Kanazawa: The Gyokusen-en and Saisetsu-Tei Roji

Ishikawa Prefecture; Edo period; strolling and tea garden; closed second week of December through to March; Gyokusen-en is located within walking distance of Kenrokuen; a local bus runs from Kanazawa JR station.

This is a combined strolling and tea garden in three sections. Gyokusen-en is named after Gyokusen-in, wife of the second Lord Maeda Toshinaga. The garden was originally

View from inside building.
Seison-Kaku Mansion.

created during the Edo period by Naokata Wakita, a chamberlain to the Kaga clan, with later work by a fourth-generation descendant Kuhei Wakita. The techniques of landscape gardening of the period are clearly demonstrated in the overall layout. The ponds, one of which is based on the Chinese character for water (*misu*), are fed by water from Kenrokuen Garden. The construction of the waterfalls and the arrangement of stones on the natural slope are designed to be enjoyed while one sits in the reception room, as well as when walking through the garden. There are forty-seven stone lanterns within the garden, including an Oribe-style, secret, Christian lantern, carved out of the valuable, blue Tomuro stone, the crafting of which was commissioned by Naokata Wakita. The image of the Virgin Mary was carved in the stem of the lantern and hidden by bushes and trees to escape the notice of the Shogunate. Other special features of this garden are the distinctive, tall, narrow *chozubachi*, with carvings of reeds which stands at the entrance to the garden. Adjacent to the tea house

Chozubachi *with Paulownia* leaves.
Gyokusen-en.

Nomura Family Samurai Garden,
with lantern protected for winter.

is a low, square, granite *chozubachi*, decorated with carvings of *Paulownia* leaves, an heirloom of the Matsudaira clan from Fukui Prefecture. Adjoining the main garden is the Saisetsu-tei Roji, which centres around a pond and inspired the poem above written by a Confucian scholar named Junan Kinoshita.

Kanazawa: Nomura Family Samurai Garden

Ishikawa Prefecture; Edo period; open most of the year, closed between 26 and 31 December; 10min local bus ride from Kanazawa JR station to Korimbo bus stop, followed by a short walk.

Nestling in a corner of the Nagamachi Samurai District of Kanazawa is a reconstruction of a traditional samurai house; most of these houses were destroyed during the demise of the feudal system. Parts of the old gate and the characteristic mud wall around the house are all that remain intact. After entering through an impressive gateway, negotiating stepping stones across the front garden and passing through the dwelling house, the rear garden can be viewed through screen openings and from a verandah running the width of the house. Beside the verandah is a particularly tall, thin *chozubachi* designed for access from the elevated position. The rear garden is of modest proportions but full of interesting features and artefacts, including several large, stone lanterns which, in winter, are given protection from frost with rice-straw coverings. Within the garden is an artificial waterfall which feeds into a pond containing koi and which creates a reflective surface, giving the impression of a much larger garden.

Uji: Byodo-in Garden

Heian period; pond garden for boating; open throughout the year; from Keihan-Sanjo station in Kyoto take the Keihan-Uji line train to Uji, approximately 40min; or by JR train from Kyoto station.

Byodo-in Temple was originally the villa of an eleventh-century prime minister. In 1052 it was converted into a Buddhist temple by his son Fujiwara Yorimichi, who was the Chief Advisor to the emperor of the day. The temple and its garden were intended to recreate the Buddhist 'Pure Land' Paradise. The major remaining building, the Phoenix Hall, dedicated to Amida Buddha, is built on an island and has an open corridor wing on each side of the main hall. The whole building is reputed to resemble a phoenix spreading its wings on its journey to Paradise. Buildings at the end of each corridor are reminiscent of fishing pavilions within *shinden*-style complexes. The predominant features of Byodo-in garden are the white gravel forecourt and the large lily pond in which the buildings are reflected. The pond was originally an inlet from the Uji River. A covered walkway traverses the pond connecting the island in the 'sea' with the 'shore', indicating that mortals can cross over to the Paradise. Refurbishment of the gardens to resemble the Heian period style more closely was carried out in 2001.

Nara: The Imperial Villa Garden Site of the Ancient Capital Nara, 'Winding Stream Garden'

Nara Prefecture; Nara period; open throughout the year except Wednesdays and the New Year holiday; from Nara station take a southbound bus to Kokkeji-mae, from where it is a short walk to the garden which is located behind the Nara Municipal Offices.

Phoenix Hall.
Byodo-in.

*Imperial Villa Garden
viewed from building.*

BELOW: *Millstone
sawatari-ishi.* Isui-en.

The remnants of the garden were discovered in 1975 during archaeological investigations on the ancient Imperial Palace site. Originally built in the Nara era (710–84), the garden is a treasured example of the gardens of the period. It was refurbished and remodelled late in the last century. A shallow, meandering stream wends its way from north to south between rocky shores on which a few sparse pines represent a windy site. Stones are laid out along the river bank, with quartz gneiss placed at the water's edge, while granite and andesite are used on the banks. The *Kyokusui-no-niwa* (Garden by the Winding Stream) is believed to have been an early setting for the ancient Heian festival, where courtiers and noblemen sit on the stream banks composing poems which they exchange for cups of sake carried on the backs of wooden ducks floating by, often accompanied by traditional music and dancing performed on a nearby stage. The garden may be viewed from a wooden building reconstructed in the early Nara style; during this period it was customary to open one side of a building by raising shutters on a 'hinge', the garden beyond being revealed and framed in a similar way to the openings formed by the sliding shutters and screens of later periods.

Nara: Isui-en Garden

Nara Prefecture; Edo and Meiji periods; strolling and tea gardens; open throughout the year except Tuesdays; from Nara station, walk northwards towards Nara Park, turn eastwards on the Kyoto road; the garden will be signposted.

The gardens of Isui-en consist of a front garden to the west of the entrance and a back garden to the east – two distinctly different gardens, built in different times. According to old temple records, the front yard was originally part of a branch temple garden, with the traditional pond and island format incorporating 'crane' and 'turtle' islands. In 1670 an influential businessman of Nara modified the garden and erected a thatched-roofed tea house from which the garden can be viewed. The rear garden, completed in 1899 by another prosperous Nara merchant, also contains a complex of streams and ponds, the largest of which has a central island with access by a distinctive, staggered, stepping-stone crossing made from reclaimed mill stones reputed to have been used in the original owner's milling business. A nearby waiting bench affords a resting place from which to contemplate the garden and the *shakkei* beyond. The garden was designed to capture a glimpse of the roof of Nandaimon Gate, with the hills of Nara beyond. Within the garden are groves of azaleas, *Nandina*, flowering cherries and plums. In the autumn a walkway of clipped *Euonymus alatus* is ablaze with colour (*see* p.88).

Nara: Yoshiki-en Garden

Nara Prefecture; Edo and Meiji periods; strolling and tea gardens; check opening times locally; located immediately next to Isui-en Garden.

Like Isui-en Garden, Yoshiki-en Garden is believed to have been the site of a high priest's residence in the seventeenth century. During the Meiji period it became privately owned and, following further building, the site was acquired by the Nara Prefectural Government in 1919, who opened it to the public in 1989. Approached by a traditional stone path and clay-tiled gateway, Yoshiki-en Garden is built on the side of a hill and consists of three different types of garden: the lower garden of the traditional pond and island style; the middle garden or 'Cedar-Moss Garden' is an open area of uncluttered design, through which a path meanders to the final garden, the 'Tea-Ceremony Garden'. At one side of the path a stone lantern stands alone, overhung by a mature *Acer palmatum* which, in full autumn colour, makes a vivid contrast with the mossy undergrowth – a simple, but distinctively Japanese feature which can be easily replicated in the West (*see* p.4).

Kyoto Outskirts: Keihanna Commemorative Park

Kyoto Prefecture; open throughout the year; take the JR train to Housono station or to Shinhousono station on the Kintetsu line, then the bus bound for 'Hikaridai 8-chome' to Keihanna Plaza, from where the garden is about a 15min walk to the east.

Keihanna Commemorative Park, built in 1994 to commemorate the 1,200th anniversary of the founding of Kyoto and covering a total area of 24.1ha (58 acres), is located on the outskirts of Kyoto near Uji. The theme of the park is 'to harmonize and coexist with nature' and consists first of a natural forest with an irrigation pond and open space for recreation, leading to a Japanese garden. This was designed to represent several aspects of traditional Japanese culture and life, including a stylized representation of rice paddies and a stroll through the countryside. An immense cluster of stones, 150m (500ft) long and 6–7m (20–23ft) high, weighing up to 70 tons each, was imported from Inujima island and designed to recreate wild nature. Although not feasible in a domestic setting, a similar effect may be achieved on a lesser scale with smaller stones. A series of stepped waterfalls creates a peaceful resting place along the route, where the movement of the water can be enjoyed at leisure. Stepping stones (*sawatari-ishi*) encourage visitors to cross the water and to become more closely involved with the natural elements.

'Wild nature' rocks.
Keihanna koen.

The Kyoto Flower Centre

The Kyoto Flower Centre is located close to Keihanna Commemorative Park; although not a garden in the traditional sense, it is a centre where a collection of exotic tropical plants is housed under glass.

In tune with the enthusiasm of the Japanese to become ever more Westernized, 'bedding' plants familiar in many parts of the world are cultivated and displayed for the admiration of visitors.

Gardens in and around Kyoto

The choice of the site of Kyoto for human settlement fulfilled a multitude of needs. Surrounded to the west, the north and the east by wooded hills, with an open plain to the south and a large central basin through which ran two rivers, the setting idealized the concept of a protective 'armchair' shape or *shinden*. Fresh water for agricultural and domestic use was, and is, in abundant supply from the two rivers which run through the valley from north to south. To the west is the Katsura River, after which one of the Imperial Villas is named, and to the east the River Kamo runs from the north-east southwards, in tune with the legend of the Blue Dragon of the East clearing the way for the White Tiger of the West. In the north-east corner of the protective hills is the revered Mount Hiei, benevolently guarding the city against evil.

Many of the early temples with their associated gardens were built on the hillsides around the city, where fresh water was available from numerous streams and cooling breezes alleviated the oppressive heat of summer. Over several centuries the central city developed from an early layout based on a Chinese grid system; this included an Imperial Palace site, administrative districts and markets. In 784, during the Heian period, Heian-Kyo, as it was then called, became the nation's capital. Following this the urban area was enlarged, with the Imperial Palace and its grounds forming a focal point at a junction of two broad boulevards. The grid system, which still remains intact, was based on precise measurements the smallest of which, *henushi*, was the lot size for a commoner; thirty-two comprised a *cho*, measuring approximately 120m (390ft) square, one or more of which was the lot size for an aristocrat or person of high rank. Within the designated areas were built dwellings, either modest or grandiose, with associated gardens of evolving styles many of which are now open for visitors to enjoy.

Public transportation around Kyoto, either by bus or train, is reasonably priced. Due to the city's geometric layout, bus and train guides are easy to follow; these may be obtained from overseas Japanese Natonal Tourist Offices or from the highly organized Tourist Offices within Kyoto itself.

Lady gardeners.
Kyoto Flower Centre.

Many of the gardens which are open to the public have generous visiting hours most of the year round, but it is advisable to check locally for the latest information. In most instances access is simply a matter of purchasing a ticket at an entrance gate. However, to visit any of the four Imperial Palace and Villa gardens it is necessary to obtain permission for a pre-booked visiting time from the Kyoto Imperial Household Agency; which is situated within the Imperial Palace grounds. For overseas visitors it is relatively easy to obtain permission for entry on the same or the next day, but it is necessary to show a passport or Alien Registration Card. Resident Japanese citizens have to wait several months to gain entry, but it is permissible for each overseas visitor to be accompanied by one Japanese person. It is also necessary to obtain written permission in advance to visit the gardens of Saiho-ji, 'The Moss Garden' (*see* below).

South-West Kyoto: Katsura Imperial Villa

Edo period; strolling and tea gardens; check conducted tour times and obtain permission from the Kyoto Imperial Household Agency; from Katsura station on the Hankyu Dentetsu Line, a 15min walk, or take the bus from Kyoto station to Katsura-Rikyu-mae bus stop, followed by a 10min walk along the river bank.

The garden of the Katsura Imperial Villa was originally commissioned by Prince Toshihito in the early seventeenth century, with later additions to the villa and the grounds being undertaken by his son Toshitada. Reputed to be one of the first gardens designed for strolling around, it became a model for the gardens of noblemen throughout the Edo period and has retained a uniqueness which may still be enjoyed. It is centred around a large, free-form pond, resulting in a perimeter path of maximum length and interest for the available space. Progressing through the garden, various scenes are revealed, some expressing literary or artistic images; of these some were based on the eleventh-century novel the *Tales of Genji*, which describes the aristocratic life of the time. Scattered through the garden are meticulously designed tea houses, built of the finest materials, from which glimpses of the garden can be enjoyed through open shutters. Numerous carved lanterns light the meandering pathways at night. Stone pathways and stepping stones, varying in design from the informal to the formal, focus the attention and direct the visitor towards a rock or plant grouping, an open view or to one of the many and various bridges.

Adjoining the main building is a bamboo terrace (*tsukimidia*) from which the August moon and its reflection on the water can be viewed and contemplated.

South-West Kyoto: Saiho-ji Temple Garden (the 'Moss Garden'; Kokedera)

Nishikyo Ward; Kamakura period; strolling garden; from Kyoto station take Kyoto Bus No.73 to Koke-dera or the train on the Hankyu Irashiyama Line to Kami-Katsura station, followed by a 15min walk.

To experience the gardens of the Saiho-ji Temple, it is necessary to obtain written permission in advance from the abbot at 56 Kamigaya-cho, Matsuo, Nishigyo-ku, Kyoto 615; tourist information offices, or hotels in Japan may be able to help. There is a substantial fee to be paid on entry and it is required that all visitors participate in a Buddhist ceremony where sutras are chanted and guests are invited to copy the manuscript. This was originally the villa site of Prince Shotoku. In the later Tempyo era (729–49), Saiho-ji was erected to enshrine three images representing the Amitabha Divinities, said to have been carried in by Gyogi Bosatsu who has been revered as the founder of the temple complex. In the fourteenth century the Zen priest Muso Kokushi took up residence in Saiho-ji, restoring some of the buildings as well as designing and constructing the gardens. The garden is built on two levels; the lower in the classical 'Pure Land' pond and island style, with paths around a pond shaped like the Japanese character for heart (*kokoro*). The groves of carefully trained maples and the moss-covered islands which they occupy, together with the rustic bridges joining the islands to the shore, are reflected in the mirror-like pond. The local clay soil, shade from the overhanging trees and high humidity have encouraged the numerous mosses which have spread, resulting in a vibrant, velvety carpet which covers most of the garden. The mosses are at their most lush during the rainy season in May and June; however, the combination of mosses and colourful autumn foliage is captivating in the late autumn. The upper level of the garden is an early example of a *kare-sansui* garden, with moss-clad stones reminiscent of a mountain waterfall. This rock-setting is reputed to have been a transitional prototype for many later dry waterfall compositions (*see* p.28).

Pond and reflections.
Katsura Imperial Villa.

Tea house in the woods. Saiho-ji Temple Garden.

BELOW: Pond and island garden. Matsuo Grand Shrine.

South-West Kyoto: Matsuo Grand Shrine Garden

Arashiyama Miya-Machi, south-west Kyoto, Nishikyo Ward; Meiji era; check locally for opening times; by Kyoto bus to Matsuo-daisha-mae stop, from where there is a short walk, or by train on the Hankyu Arashiyama Line to Matsuo station, with a short walk to the west.

The Matsuo Grand Shrine is one of the oldest shrines in Kyoto and was built when dwellers along the base of the city's western hill range began worshipping the divine spirits of the Matsuo Hill as their guardian gods. In 701 the influential Shin family from Korea erected a shrine on the site to be worshipped as a protector of agriculture, building and construction, spinning and dyeing and of personal safety; brewers of

Kare-sansui and pond garden. Tenryu-ji Temple.

sake worship at the shrine as the originator of all brewing. The original garden has been dated between 1570 and 1590. However, the gardens which can be seen today were designed in the twentieth century by Mirei Shigemori and are regarded as one of the most artistic works of landscape construction since the beginning of the Meiji era. The Showa New Garden has three main parts; unusual walkways of pebbles set in black mortar lead visitors through the site, a modern, mirror-like pond and island garden with well-defined stone edging, reflects the hallowed hillside and the shrine building. A dense planting of *Sasa veitchii* clothes the hillside, interspersed with upright stones, depicting the gods of the mountain. A side garden in modern *kare-sansui* style, backed with bamboo fencing, is a significant feature of the Matsuo-daisha Shrine garden.

South-West Kyoto: Tenryu-ji Temple Garden

Ukyo-ku Ward; Kamakura period; strolling garden; open throughout the year; by train, 2min walk from Arashiyama station on the Keifuku Dentetsu Line, or JR Sagano Line to Saga station; several Kyoto buses run from Kyoto station and other parts of the city.

Originally dating from the fourteenth century, the pond garden was created for enjoyment on foot or to be viewed from the verandah of the abbot's quarters. The three horizontal elements of dry sand garden adjacent to the verandah, the pond with associated rock groupings and the inclusion in the design of the distant mountains of Arashiyama and Kameyama together create an illusion of depth. Tenryu-ji is an early surviving example of the technique of *shakkei* – borrowed scenery.

The rock groupings include the *Ryumon-no-taki*, the 'Dragon Gate Waterfall', with carp stone, depicting the legend that 'if a carp can climb the waterfall, it will turn into a dragon and enter heaven', an allusion to the Buddhist belief in man's struggle to attain enlightenment. Another symbolic rock grouping is of seven, vertically positioned rocks, depicting the legendary Mount Horai where, it was believed, those who attained immortality lived together in perfect harmony.

The Arashiyama district of Kyoto is renowned for cherry blossoms in the spring and for the autumn colouring of maples. In November a festival is held in which colourful boats float on the Arashiyama River, with musicians and singers dressed in costume performing traditional pieces.

South-West Kyoto: Umekoji Koen Project

Umekoji district; strolling garden; open throughout the year, but closed on Mondays; located a 15min walk due west of Kyoto JR station, or by Kyoto bus from Kyoto station and other parts of the city.

Umejoki Koen covers an area of 11.6ha (5 acres) which was once a major Japan Railways freight yard. Built in 1994 in celebration of the city's 1,200th-year anniversary, as part of Kyoto's Greenery Campaign, it is the largest park to be built in Kyoto for several hundred years and includes an area of open lawn for recreation, as well as a short length of railway track on which runs the oldest steam train in the city. In a corner of the park is 'The Garden of the Suzaku' (*Suzaku no Niwa*), which was built on contaminated land,

A walk through the countryside.
Suzaku no Niwa.

Glimpse of a temple garden.
Myoshin-ji.

bordered by the railway line, commercial buildings and apartment houses. The design aims were to create a new style which enhances the community life of Kyoto, at the same time avoids imitating traditional gardens while inviting visitors into the tranquil world of nature. Great care was taken in choosing the trees, stones and other elements of the garden to create a haven of peace separate from daily city life. The aim of the garden is to depict life in Japan and the design includes an elevated walk through the mountains with autumnal tints (*momiji-dani*) and a representation of Japanese red pine woods. A contrasting field along a river or road (*nosoji*) is woven into the perimeter walkway. Modern designs are used for the distinctive water themes, especially the *mizukagami*, a water surface mirror with stepping-stone crossing, which attempts to convey the unexpectedness of a world unrelated to reality (*see* p.47).

North-West Kyoto: Myoshin-ji

North-west Kyoto, Ukyo Ward; Kamakura period; temple complex with numerous gardens; open daily; check locally for individual garden opening times and permissions; by local bus to Myoshin-ji-mae bus stop, by train on JR San-in Line to Hanazono station, with a short walk northwards, or on the Keifuku Electric Railway, Kitano Line to Myoshin-ji station and walk southwards.

North-West Kyoto: Taizo-in Temple within Myoshin-ji Complex

Muromachi and Meiji periods; open throughout the year.

Kare-sansui *garden,*
Taizo-in.

BELOW: *Pond and island*
garden. Ryoan-ji Temple.

The original *kare-sansui* garden at Taizo-in was built in the late fifteenth–early sixteenth century, reputedly designed by Kano Motonobu, a skilled painter of sepia landscapes. The garden can be seen as a representation of that painting technique. Layers of tall trees, a bamboo grove and varied rock settings create the impression of a larger landscape through which flows a dry stream with Mount Horai symbolized by turtle and crane 'Isles of the Blest', connected by stone bridges.

A modern *kare-sansui* garden, with stone settings in honey-coloured gravel raked into deep 'eddies', contrasts with the earlier style. Unusually, the visitor may walk through the two parts of this garden. A larger, modern garden designed by Nakane Kinsaku and created on the hillside below the temple, is a landscape through which visitors may also walk. The central theme is a fast-flowing waterfall and stream with rock settings and massed azalea plantings. The optimal view of the garden is from the bottom looking up towards the watercourse and rustic arbour.

North-West Kyoto: Ryoan-ji Temple

Ryoan-ji Ward; Muromachi period; *kare-sansui* and pond garden; open throughout the year; by Kyoto or JR bus to Ryoanji-mae stop, from where it is a short walk.

The fame and popularity of the rock garden attract hordes of visitors, not all of whom sense or respect the peace and tranquillity created by it. For a peaceful experience, it is advisable to visit the garden in the early morning or late afternoon, and during school term time. Situated in the foothills north-west of the city, the rock garden at Ryoan-ji is one of the most famous in Japan, if not the world. Originally constructed in about 1500, fifteen rocks are arranged in the classic two, three and five settings in a 'sea' of greyish white gravel. Colonies of moss soften the interface between rocks and gravel, bringing a modicum of colour to the otherwise monochrome composition. It is tempting to try and interpret the 'message' that the designer intended: could the stones symbolize a mother tiger and her cubs swimming in the sea? Could it be the tops of clouds in the sky? Perhaps there is no story to the design and it was meant as a *kōan*, a technique whereby Zen priests attempt to provoke thought in their students. Viewed from the temple verandah, a mud wall, topped with a shingle and tiled roof, forms the backdrop to the stone composition (*see* p.31). In contrast, behind and above the wall trees sway gently in the breeze, with cherry blossoms in the spring and colourful foliage in the autumn. Maintaining the gravel in pristine condition is a daily task, undertaken with pride by the monks to whom it is a vehicle aiding contemplation of, and communion with, the natural world. The rock garden at Ryoan-ji is a small part of larger grounds which were originally the estate of a noble family in the Heian period. A pond and island garden with circumferential path adjoins the more famous rock garden and provides a quiet stroll through the trees and beside the lily-filled pond.

North-West Kyoto: Kinkaku-ji Temple (The Golden Pavilion)

Kinusaga Ward; Kamakura period; pond and island garden; open all year; by city bus to Kinkaku-ji-mae bus stop.

Situated in the north-western foothills, 'The Villa of the Northern Hills' (*Kitayama dono*) was modified in the early 1390s into a personal retreat for Shogun Ashikaga Yoshimitsu, who renamed it *Rokuon-ji*, 'Temple of the Deer Park', after the famous park where Guatama Buddha delivered his first sermon after his enlightenment. Today the palace is called *Kinkaku-ji*, 'Temple of the Golden Pavilion', after the three-storey, gilded pavilion built in the Chinese style, on an island in the main pond. The garden was designed to be appreciated from the water or inside the building, but access for the average visitor is limited to a small path which winds its way around the pond. The positioning of the islands and the associated plantings gives an illusion of space, enhanced by the inclusion of a distant view of Mount Kinugasa, a skilful example of *shakkei*. It is a garden full of interest and surprises, not least of which is an early *kare-sansui* garden in which stands an intricately pruned and trained pine in the shape of a junk under sail, a remnant of Chinese influence, perhaps. In early November, when the maples are showing their most glorious autumn colouring, the garden of *Kinkaku-ji* is one of those selected for evening opening. Hues of red,

Gateway to the Golden Temple.
Kinkaku-ji.

orange and yellow are floodlit and, on occasion, live music is performed. Check locally for special events.

North-West Kyoto: Koetsu-ji

Takagamine Ward; Edo period; strolling and tea garden; open throughout the year except from 10 to 13 November; by City bus (No.1 *kita* [north]), to Takagamine-Genkoan-mae stop, then a 3min walk westwards.

Situated in the north-western foothills, Koetsu-ji Temple was originally a home for the artist Hon-ami Koetsu, built on land donated to him by the shogun Tokugawa Ieyasu in 1615, which became an established artists' colony. Koetsu was an accomplished calligrapher, potter and metalworker as well as being a renowned tea master. The entrance to the garden is approached via a distinctive stone path lined with maples. Within the garden are several tea houses, connected by winding paths overhung with maples. The inner garden of the Taikyo-an tea house is separated from the main area by the most famous element of the garden, a long-low, curving fence of diagonal bamboo forming diamond shapes and tied with traditional black hemp knots, with precisely cut bamboo bound along the top to give protection from the elements. It is reputed that the original fence was designed by Koetsu and represents 'a cow lying down in a field'. Due to its location, Koetsu-ji is often shrouded in mist, giving it an ethereal feel, particularly in autumn as one looks out towards the distant wooded hills.

Entrance path in the rain.
Koetsu-ji.

North-West Kyoto: Shoden-ji

Kita-ku; Edo period; *kare-sansui* garden; open throughout the year; by City bus (No.1 *kita*) from Kitaoji bus terminal in the north of Kyoto to Jinko-in-mae, from where there is a short walk to the north-west.

Located on a peaceful hillside to the north-west of busy Kyoto City, the unique design of the garden of Shoden-ji Temple has a special atmosphere. Viewed from the temple verandah, the *kare-sansui* garden is enclosed with tile-topped, mud walls which are painted white. Unlike the familiar rock settings of other gardens, the 'islands in the sea' of white sand are clusters of large azaleas in traditional groupings of three, five and seven, the odd numbers providing a harmonious, yet asymmetrical composition. The azaleas are clipped in the characteristic *karikomi* style to resemble weather-worn rocks. Above the walls can be seen the native woodland, the apparent randomness of which contrasts with the simplicity and geometry of the small garden. In the background, a distant glimpse of Mount Hiei to the east is employed in the technique of *shakkei* – borrowed scenery – which takes the eye beyond the boundaries of the garden. Due to its location, Shoden-ji has few visitors and is an ideal place for quiet contemplation, which is at its best on a clear day, when the distant views can be enjoyed, particularly in autumn when the leaves are turning and in spring when the azaleas are in flower.

North-East Kyoto: Entsu-ji Temple Garden

Hataeda village, Iwakura area; early Edo period; *kare-sansui* garden; open throughout the year; by City bus from Kitaoji terminal to Entsuji-michi, from where there is a short walk westwards.

Originally the site of an Imperial villa, later becoming a Zen temple, Entsu-ji Temple is situated in the northern hills. The tranquil garden is designed to be viewed from the main temple hall and verandah. A low, clipped hedge forms a well-defined boundary to the north, east and south. The natural woodland of *Cryptomeria japonica*, acers and bamboos surrounds the site and is carefully managed so that Mount Hiei can be seen in the distance, skilfully employing the technique of *shakkei*. Within and below the hedge line are groupings of horizontally set stones which are reputed to be naturally occurring outcroppings, softened with low plantings. In contrast to the more familiar sands and gravels which form the horizontal plain of most *kare-sansui* gardens, the forefront at Entsu-ji is moss-covered giving the appearance of a luxuriant carpet. The composition of the flat, horizontal surface, with random rocky outcrops, is punctuated by the formally clipped hedge to create the low, mostly horizontal, foreground. The middle ground moves from spreading trees to vertical trunks, which lead the eye towards

*Western corner.
Shoden-ji.*

BELOW: Moss-covered
kare-sansui. *Entsu-ji.*

Mount Hiei in the background. If possible, plan a visit to Entsu-ji on a clear day, preferably in the autumn when the turning foliage is highlighted against a clear blue sky.

North-East Kyoto: Renge-ji

Kamitakano Ward; early Edo period; pond and island garden; open throughout the year; by train on the Eizan Line electric railway to Miyakehachiman station, cross the river by nearby bridge, then turn right.

Approaching the temple building at Renge-ji is a stone path and a geometric garden with an overhanging, ancient *Ginkgo biloba*. On either side of the path are unusual twin lanterns, which are named after the temple. The firebox of the Renge-ji lanterns is taller and thinner than that of most of the other styles and somewhat resembles a closed toadstool. The pond garden at Renge-ji is designed to be viewed from the main hall of the *shoin*. The nearby hillside provides a backdrop to the composition as well as water to feed the central pond, in which the surrounding rocks and plantings are reflected. A distinctive, turtle-shaped rock appears to be moving towards the bank.

'Turtle' rock.
Renge-ji.

BELOW: *View of pond
and island garden from*
Runin-tei. *Shugaku-in
Imperial Villa.*

Around the perimeter of the pond are arranged numerous rocks, complemented by formally clipped shrubs. A simple stone bridge crosses the water, which is overhung with nodding maple branches. When in full leaf the foliage all but hides lanterns on the distant shore. A quiet garden, on the outskirts of Kyoto, Renge-ji is at its best during the autumn when the maples are turning yellow, red and orange, and the ancient ginkgo is resplendent in its golden mantle.

North-East Kyoto: *Shugaku-in Imperial Villa*

Shugaku-in District; Edo period; strolling garden; check conducted tour times and obtain permission from the Kyoto Imperial Househould Agency in the grounds of the Imperial Palace; by City bus No.5 or No.5 North (*kita*) to Shugaku-in-Rikyu-michi stop, then a 15min walk up hill, or by Eizan Electric Railway Eizan Line, to Shugaku-in station and then walk up hill.

The Imperial Villa gardens of Shugaku-in in the foothills of Mount Hiei were built in the seventeenth century, by ex-Emperor Gomuzuno-o, with financial assistance from the ruling Tokugawa shogunate. Although not used a permanent residence, the retired Emperor visited it many times during his remaining years. It is reputed that the retired emperor designed the gardens himself, following the style of Kobori Enshu, who had been involved in the design of the gardens of Sento Gosho, in the grounds of the Kyoto Imperial Palace. Within the extensive site are three distinct gardens, located at different levels on the hillside, each containing a tea house and each taking advantage of the view of distant hills in the time-honoured technique of *shakkei*. Within the complex are many transitions from one part of the gardens to another, negotiated via traditional wooden and bamboo-covered gateways set among heavy bamboo protective fences or colour-washed mud walls topped with grey tiles, typical of the period. Pathways and bridges direct visitors through the gardens, crossing paddy fields and vegetable plots bounded by heavily pruned shrubs and pine trees. Bridges vary in style from simple wooden structures to the ornate *Chitose-bashi*, 'Bridge of a Thousand Years', joining two islands in the Upper Garden pond which was formed by damming the Tanigawa River. Streams flow swiftly from the Upper to the Lower gardens tumbling over waterfalls, large and small. From the topmost point of the garden, adjacent to the *Rinun-tei* tea house, there is a magnificent view over the Upper pond, with its meticulously pruned 'pines' and maples, reflected in the mirror-like water, with views of the hills beyond.

North-East Kyoto: Manshu-in Temple Garden

Sakyo-Ku District; Edo period; *kare-sansui* garden; open throughout the year; City bus No.5 or No.5 North (*kita*), to Ichijo-ji-Shimizu-cho stop, from where there is 15min walk uphill, or take the Eizan Electric Railway, Eizan Line, to Shugaku-in station, followed by a 15min walk uphill.

Located in the north-eastern foothills, a short walk from Shugaku-in and founded in the eighth century by Dengyo Daishi, Manshu-in was originally located in the northern valley of the Saito region of Mount Hiei. At the beginning of the Edo period the temple was moved to the present site by Prince Ryosho, whose knowledge and creativity are reflected in the plan of the garden as well as in the architectural style of the building, which is typical of the *shoin* style and from where the garden can be viewed; this may be compared with the Katsura Detached Villa. The predominant feature of the garden is the raked, white gravel 'pond' in which are situated several islands. From an artificial 'mountain' and Mount Horai rock formation, a dry stream flows under a stone bridge into the dry pond garden. Unusual representations of crane and turtle islands can be contemplated from the verandah of the *shoin*. Although there are some rock placings, the main formations are created by heavily clipped azaleas, together with skilfully trained and pruned *Pinus pentaphylla*, one of which is over 400 years old and represents a crane in flight. In the past there was another in the shape of a turtle. The garden is bounded by the nearby hillside, with plantings of overhanging maples and more formal 'pine' trees.

'Turtle' island. Manshu-in.

North-East Kyoto: Shisen-do Hermitage Garden

Ichijo-ji District; Edo period; strolling garden; open throughout the year; take City Bus No.5 to Ichijo-ji-Sagari-matsu-cho stop, followed by a short walk up the hill, or by Eizan Electric Railway, Eizan Line to Ichijo-ji station, walk eastwards, crossing Shirakawa-dori, and up hill to the Shisen-do Temple.

Situated at the foot of the northern mountain range of Higashiyama, the Ichijo-ji district still maintains something of a country village atmosphere. The Hermitage of Shisen-do was built in 1641 by Jozan Ishikawa, a one-time samurai warrior, who chose to pursue a quieter life as a scholar of the Chinese classics and a landscape architect. The *kare-sansui* garden is first glimpsed from within the dark building. Sliding screens open on to the long verandah, framing the expanse of raked white sand and clipped azaleas in the formal *o-karikomi* style. In autumn the evergreen foliage of the azaleas contrasts with the vibrant reds, oranges and yellows of the overhanging maples. Visitors are invited to put on soft slippers, and cross the *kare-sansui* garden towards stone steps which pass through more clipped azaleas on the way to a lower garden in which a stream fed by mountain water runs into a small pond. Running water also provides the power for a *shishi-odoshi* hidden among the boundary plantings, its rhythmical 'clack-clack' being reminiscent of earlier times when there were wild animals to be deterred from the garden. Interesting and unusual features in Shisen-do include a *tsukubai* grouping and bamboo sleeve fence adjacent to the main verandah. Of particular note is a small upper room with a dormer-like roof and shuttered window added to building in the eighteenth century so that the abbess-in-residence could commune with the moon.

*Moon-viewing window.
Shisen-do.*

North-East Kyoto: Ginkaku-ji (Jisho-ji)

Sanyo-ku District; Muromachi period; strolling garden and *kare-sansui*; open throughout the year; by City bus, of which there are several, to Ginkaku-ji mae stop, from where there is a short walk to the east.

Located on the lower slopes of Higashiyama mountain to the north-east of the city, the original temple complex and garden were built in the mid fifteenth century as a country retreat and retirement home for Ashikaga Yoshimasa, the eighth Ashikaga Shogun. He was the grandson of the builder of the Golden Pavilion, Kinkaku-ji, and intended to cover the pavilion at Ginkaku-ji with silver leaf. However, this was never accomplished. Following his death in 1490 the complex became a temple for Zen Buddhism. The design of the garden was loosely based on that at Saiho-ji, with a lower garden for strolling around a pond and an early dry garden stone grouping on the mossy hillside which overlooks the temple buildings and the lower garden. A later edition to the garden, probably in the Edo period, is a distinctive *kare-sansui*, in which a raised area of silver sand, *ginshanada*, 'silver sand, open sea', was made to reflect the moonlight and to enhance the appreciation of the garden during moonlit evenings. Beside the 'silver sea' is the *kogetsudai*, 'platform facing the moon', which is a conically-shaped pile of silver sand with a flat surface, stylistically representing Mount Fuji (*see* p.30). There are several small gardens within the temple complex, including *kare-sansui* with stone groupings, typical of those intended for contemplation from within a building. A well-known feature of the gardens at Ginkaku-ji is the distinctive water basin (*chozubachi*), which, although of an early design, has a twentieth-century appearance, shaped like a cube, with carved lattice patterns on all four vertical sides. Copies are often used in domestic gardens, however, the weight needs to be borne in mind.

North-East Kyoto: Hakusasonsō Garden

Sakyo-ku; Taisho/Showa periods; tea garden; open throughout the year; by City bus, of which there are several, to Ginkaku-ji-mae stop, from where there is a short walk to the east.

Located just to the west of Ginkaku-ji, Hakusasonsō Villa garden was built in the early twentieth century by the Japanese-style painter Hashimoto Kansetsu. Within the garden is the artist's studio, in which are housed collections of Greek and Persian pottery, Chinese clay figures, Indian miniatures and Japanese and Chinese paintings and calligraphies, as well as Kansetsu's own paintings. A naturalistic pond is the central focus of the garden, beside which a rustic tea house nestles under overhanging maple trees. The garden can be viewed from a small verandah which protrudes over the water. Access to the tea house (*keijakuan*) is by elevated and graduated stepping stones, which concentrate the mind and refocus thoughts so that the garden may be fully appreciated. There are other stone groupings throughout the garden, as well as lanterns, bridges and pagodas. Transitions within the garden are made through several unassuming gateways, with shingle and thatched roofs. Hakusasonsō is a fine example of the creation of peace and tranquillity in a busy urban setting.

North-East Kyoto: Philosopher's Path (Tetsugakuno-michi)

Sanyo-ku; open throughout the year; by City bus to Ginkaku-ji-mae stop, from where there is a short walk to the east.

ABOVE: *Ginkaku-ji style* chozubachi. *Ginkaku-ji Temple.*

RIGHT: *Tea house beside the water. Hakusasonsō.*

The northern entrance to the Philosopher's Path is located between Hakusasonsō Garden and Ginkaku-ji. Stretching for 2km (1¼ miles) between Ginkaku-ji and Nyakuo-ji Shrine, it follows the route of a canal at the base of the Higashiyama foothills. The philosopher Nishida Kitaro meditated as he walked along the path which was named after him. One side of the path is bordered by the back fences and walls of Kyoto houses, while on the other, overhanging the canal, is an avenue of trees which make the path popular to visitors all year round, but especially in spring for the cherry blossoms, in early summer for the fireflies and in autumn for the foliage colouring. A short walk from the southern end of the Philosopher's Path is the Nanzen-ji Temple complex with its many gardens; the Path may also be approached from this end (by city bus No.5 or No.100, to Nanzenji-Eikando-michi, from where it is a short walk.

South-East Kyoto: Konchi-in Garden of Nanzen-ji Temple

Sakyo-ku; Edo period; *kare-sansui* and pond garden; open throughout the year; by City bus to Eikando-mae or Hosho-jicho bus stop, from where it is a short walk, or by Kyoto City subway (*chikatetsu*) on the Tozai Line to Kaege station, from where it is a short walk to the north-east.

During the restoration of the temple in the early seventeenth century, the eminent priest Ishin Suden commissioned Kobori Enshu to design and construct the temple building and *kare-sansui* garden south of the abbot's quarters (*hojo*). Partly due to the status of Enshu as an accomplished designer, the garden of Konchi-in is one of the most celebrated in Kyoto. The dry landscape garden has a sloping backdrop of *o-karikomi* shrubs and heavily pruned trees. Nestling in the large

Philosopher's Path.

Kare-sansui and curving path. Konchi-in.

flat area of raked white sand are symbolic 'turtle' and 'crane' islands, constructed from stone groupings and associated plantings. Although designed to be viewed from the verandah, the garden of Konchi-in can be glimpsed only in part at any one time. Through the open screens a more recent, curving, stepping-stone path invites the viewer to enter the garden in spirit if not in person. Of a later period than Enshu is a small garden, east of the *hojo*, which is in the shape of the Japanese character for heart (*kokoro*), enhanced with stone settings and plantings. Visitors can walk through this part of the garden to reach the Toshogu Shrine, dedicated to Tokugawa Ieyasu, the benefactor of Nanzen-ji.

South-East Kyoto: Daigo Sanpo-in Temple

Fushimi-Ku, Kyoto; Momoyama period; garden for viewing from inside a building; open throughout the year; by City bus from Keihan-Sanjo terminal to Sanpo-in-mae stop, from where there is a short walk.

There has been a grand temple on the site in the foothills of Mount Daigo since the tenth century. In common with many other architectural treasures, the buildings suffered during the fifteenth-century civil war. At the end of the sixteenth century the military ruler of Japan Toyotomi Hideyoshi undertook

the restoration of the buildings and the creation of pleasure gardens, most famously in 1598 holding a sumptuous cherry-viewing party on the site. During the subsequent twenty years the garden was developed with the importing of some 700 stones, some of great value. The central feature of the garden is a Mount Horai rock composition, from which a wooden plank bridge leads to a 'crane' island; a stone bridge leads to the 'turtle' island. The upper *kare-sansui* garden includes a double-gourd motif of moss set in white gravel, symbolizing luck and longevity. Although the gardens at Sanpo-in were originally designed for strolling through and to enjoy on foot, viewing is now limited to the temple verandahs. A comfortable vantage point can be found on the wooden steps leading from the temple to the garden.

Central Kyoto: Gardens of Daitoku-ji Temple Complex

Kita-ku, Daitoku-ji Cho; *kare-sansui* gardens; check locally for opening times, some gardens are open to the public throughout the year, others only on certain days, for the more private gardens written permission may be necessary; by City bus (there are several) to Daitoku-ji mae stop, from where there is a short walk northwards.

Jason Hayter

Unfortunately, photography is not permitted within the Sanpo-in complex. On a cold November afternoon in 1997 the author was admiring the garden, when another visitor arrived; seating himself on the temple steps, he began to sketch the garden and temple buildings; a brief conversation ensued, followed by contact several years later. The accompanying illustration is a copy of the sketch made that day by Jason Hayter, who was an architectural student in Kyoto at the time. All the other illustrations in this book have been prepared by Jason.

The Daitoku-ji Temple complex in the north of the city centre was founded in the early fourteenth century by Shuho Myocho. It is the headquarters of the Daitoku-ji branch of the Rinzai Zen sect. The original buildings were destroyed by fires in 1453 and 1468 and then later rebuilt under the patronage of a rich merchant from Osaka. From the sixteenth to the eighteenth century numerous sub-temples were built within the complex, many of which were destroyed during anti-Buddhist disturbances following the Meiji Restoration. However, some twenty temples are still in existence, most classified as national treasures and important cultural properties. The sub-temples within the complex consist of several rooms connected by passageways, some of which are external to the building and protected by overhanging roofs, forming verandahs from which garden scenes can be appreciated. The areas available for the creation of gardens are small, rectangular spaces contained within the perimeter boundaries of the building and the surrounding protective walls. Within such confines many ancient *kare-sansui* gardens have inspired scholars and laymen for centuries.

Central Kyoto: Daisen-in at Daitoku-ji

Muromachi period; *kare-sansui*; open throughout the year.

There are two parts to the gardens at Daisen-in: to the south of the *hojo* is a small garden consisting mostly of white gravel raked into patterns, with two white gravel cones, typical of the period. To the north and east of the building is one of the most famous gardens in Japan which,

in a very small space, depicts a stream flowing from remote mountains towards the sea. Meticulously pruned trees accompany large, carefully chosen rocks to portray the mountain scene, with 'water' which flows under the stone bridge and around islands. At the lower end of the garden in the 'sea' is a notable stone which is reputed to be a ship at sea. A small and powerful garden, Daisen-in is popular with Japanese people and visitors alike. It is advisable to choose a time when groups are unlikely to be visiting. The garden of Daisen-in Temple is described in more detail in Chapter 2.

Central Kyoto: Ryogen-in Temple at Daitoku-ji

Muromachi period; *kare-sansui* garden; open throughout the year.

The Ryogen-in Temple is one of the oldest and most important Zen Buddhist temples. It is believed to have been constructed by the priest Tokei Soboku in 1502 and included the Meditation Hall, which remains to this day. From its verandah can be viewed one of the gardens, '*Isshidan*', which was refurbished in 1980 by the priest Katsudo following the demise of an ancient tree which had been an important presence within the garden. *Isshidan* is bounded by tile-topped, mud walls. A rectangular garden contains a *Horai-san* style rock garden, where the central rock represents the sacred Mount Horai, and other rock groupings represent a 'crane' island and a mossy mound representing a 'tortoise' island, all set in a 'sea' of raked white gravel.

Hojo kare-sansui *garden. Daisen-in.*

'Isshidan' kare-sansui.
Ryogen-in.

BELOW: Tsukubai
and water containers.
Omote Senke.

The recently constructed *'Totekiko'*, reputedly the smallest stone garden in Japan, runs alongside a covered walkway. The white gravel, raked into straight lines depicting a river in flow, is broken by concentric circles around free-standing stones, which indicate that the stronger the power of any obstruction to the flow, the larger are the ripples, symbolic of man's experiences in life. To the north, the *Ryōgen-tei* garden, 'Garden of the Dragon Song', reputedly designed by Saomi in the Muromachi era, is the oldest garden in the Daitoku-ji complex. Backed by a tile-topped, colour-washed, mud wall, the moss-floored rectangular garden, probably originally covered in raked sand, includes a rock setting which is believed to represent the legendary Mount Shumi-sen, the mountain at the centre of the Buddhist world. A small *sanzon* grouping, representing the Buddhist trilogy, nestles among the lush mosses.

Central Kyoto: Omote Senke School of Tea, Fushin-an Tea Garden

Kamigyo-ku; originally Edo period; tea garden; by City bus to Kitaoji-Horikawa followed by a short walk southwards, or to Horikawa-Imedagawa and a short walk northwards, or by subway (*chikatetsu*) to Kuramaguchi station, from where walk three blocks west and turn to the south; not open to the general public, special permission is required.

The drinking of tea in Japan as an artistic pursuit was developed from the drinking of tea-powder from Sung China in 1191. Four centuries later, the Japanese ceremony had evolved and become popular among the aristocracy, powerful samurai, rich tradesmen and, in particular, Zen Buddhists. Sen-no-

Rikyu, a courtier in the sixteenth century, became the greatest master of the tea ceremony. He developed the concept of the tea garden (*roji*, dewy path) as a way of enlightenment en route to the tea house. The early tea garden at Omote-Senke was created by Rikyu and later developed by his son and grandson. The three-tatami-mat tea arbour, which stands in the garden, was constructed in 1913, following the destruction by fire of the original in 1788. Typical of tea garden design, the garden is sub-divided into an outer and an inner *roji*, each of which houses water basins and waiting booths, as well as a well beside the bamboo *agesudo* gateway, which marks the transition between the parts of the garden. Passage through the peaceful inner garden is by raised stepping stones (*tobi-ishi*), which focuses the mind and prepares guests for participation in the spirituality of the ceremony (*see* pp.34–5).

Stone 'beach'.
Sento Gosho.

BELOW: *Corner of the 'Tiger Glen Garden' from*
inside the Daishoin Hall. Nishi-Hongan-ji.

Central Kyoto: Sento Gosho Garden

Kamigyo-Ku; early Edo period; strolling garden; by City bus to Karasuma-Marutamuchi, from where there is a short walk northwards, or by Karasuma subway to Marutamuchi station, from where there is also a short walk northwards; check locally for official tour times; permission needs to be obtained from the Kyoto Imperial Household Agency Office near to the Imperial Palace.

The original gardens of Sento Palace were smaller than they are today, divided by a wall from the adjoining garden of Omiya Palace. The two palaces were built in the seventeenth century for Emperor Gomizuno-o, who abdicated, and his successor the Empress Tofukumon-in. In 1854 Sento Palace suffered several fires and was not rebuilt since there was no retired emperor alive at the time. However, the Omiya Palace was rebuilt and is still used on occasion to accommodate the Imperial family when visiting Kyoto or receiving visiting heads of state. The wall dividing the two gardens was removed and the result modified to become one large strolling garden. It is believed that the gardens were originally designed by Kobori Enshu in the seventeenth century but, after modifications, now bear little resemblance to his design. Within the garden are two ponds, with perimeter paths and linking bridges of several styles, from the simple rustic to the elaborate, wisteria clad, zigzag bridge which provides changing views of the garden. The original bridge was of wood and earth and also built in the seventeenth century and rebuilt twice since. The imposing stone bridge was constructed in the middle of the Meiji era at the end of the nineteenth century. On strolling around the garden, details and vistas are revealed, not the least of which is a sizeable stone 'beach' along the shoreline of the Southern Pond. Nearby is the tea pavilion – *seika-tei* – from where visitors enjoyed the garden while partaking of fine food, tea and sake.

Central Kyoto: Nishi-Hongan-ji

Shimogyo-Ku; Momoyama period; *kare-sansui* garden; check locally for opening times; a short walk to the north and west of Kyoto JR station or by local bus from other parts of the city.

The temple complex of Nishi-Hongan-ji in the heart of Kyoto includes superb examples of Momoyana architecture, some of which were moved to the present site from the Momoyama Castle site to the south-east of Kyoto. The ornate Karamon Gate, built in the Chinese style, is a Japanese national treasure, as is the Daishoin Hall, which contains a large collection of sliding panel paintings. The *Kokei-no-niwa*, 'Tiger-Glen', garden is situated to the east of the Daishoin Hall and was designed to be viewed from the long verandah or through the openings revealed when the sliding doors are pulled back. The name 'Tiger-Glen' derives from a powerful rock setting in the north-east corner, reputed to be the dwelling of a benevolent tiger. Included in the grouping is a dry waterfall (*kare-taki*) from which flows a stream of white gravel, negotiating its way between 'crane' and 'turtle' islands which are connected by two large stone bridges. The sombreness of the 'Tiger-Glen' garden is accentuated by the predominant plantings of cycads, their heavy, dark-green foliage giving a mysterious feel to the enclosed garden. In winter the contrast is accentuated, when the fronds of the cycads are wrapped in honey-coloured rice straw as protection against low temperatures.

ishi, 'steps across the marsh', which meander through the water lilies. The large, circular stones were formerly supports for the sixteenth-century Gojo Bridge which crossed the nearby Kamo River until it was destroyed in an earthquake. To the east, the largest garden is dominated by a large pond with 'crane' and 'turtle' islands and a Chinese-style covered bridge (*taihekaku*), with a magnificent shingle-roofed centrepiece. The garden may be viewed from seats on the bridge and the terrapins languishing in the sun on the free-standing rocks observed. The Heian Shrine garden can be enjoyed at all times of the year with sequences of plant accents from cherry blossoms in spring to colourful foliage in autumn.

Central Kyoto: Heian Shrine

Sakyo-ku, Okazaki Nishi; Meiji period; strolling garden; open throughout the year; by City bus No.5 to Bijutsukan-mae stop, or by the Tozai subway line to Higashiyama station, from where there is a short walk.

Built in 1895 to commemorate Kyoto's 1,100th anniversary and as a shrine to the city's founder Emperor Kammu. The site is a scale reconstruction of the original Imperial Palace built in 794. The gardens of the shrine follow the basic design of a Heian-period pond and island garden, with the addition of more recently introduced plants and design techniques. In the western garden is a large grove of cherry and willow trees; distinctive, latticed bamboo structures support the ancient weeping cherry trees, which can be admired from all angles in spring. The northern part of the garden includes a large pond with rocky islands, the largest of which houses a stone pagoda and can be reached by the *sawatari-*

Central Kyoto: Murin-an

Sakyo-ku, Kusagawa-cho; Meiji period; strolling and tea garden; open throughout the year, except between 29 December and 3 January; by City bus No.5 to Hoshojicho bus stop, from where there is a short walk; or by Tozai subway line to Keage station, with a short walk to the north and west.

The tranquil garden of Murin-an begins to move away from the traditional formality of earlier Japanese gardens. Built in 1896 in the Higashiyama foothills by Aritomo Yamagata, a military veteran and forward-thinking prince, although respecting the traditions of Japanese garden design his ideas leaned towards a more naturalistic feel – an inclination shared by the experienced designer Ogawa Jihei who laid out the garden. Effectively taking advantage of the technique of *shakkei*, the unusually flat and open garden of Murin-an appears to be much larger than it actually is. At the further end, a three-tier

Murin-an garden from inside the tea house.

waterfall feeds water into a stream and rapids, eventually slowing down into two open ponds. The water is diverted through pipes and culverts from nearby Lake Biwa, giving the impression of a naturally flowing source from the hills behind. A large expanse of the garden is of lush grass through which a shallow stream flows, meandering between horizontal rocks and simple plantings. As well as a tea house and traditional wooden-structure house within the gardens, there is a two-storey Western-style house; it was in this that, in 1903, the political leaders of Japan met to discuss the foreign policy of Japan just before the Russo-Japanese war, a meeting which took its name from the site: the Conference of Murin-an.

Central Kyoto: Kodai-ji

Higashiyama-Ku; Edo period; strolling and tea gardens; open throughout the year; by City bus No.206, to Higashiyama-yasui stop, from where it is a short walk.

Kodai-ji Temple is located in the foothills of the Higashiyama mountains to the south-east of Kyoto. Originally established in 1605 as a memorial to her husband by the widow of Shogun Toyotomi Hideyoshi, most of the cost was provided by Tokugawa Ieyasu, who later became Shogun of Japan. The high standard of design and construction of the buildings and gardens established Kodai-ji as an important sub-temple of the Kennin-ji Temple complex. Following extensive fires in 1789, only a few of the buildings remained. However, they were well preserved and have all been designated 'Important Cultural Properties' by the government. The Temple Garden at Kodai-ji was redesigned by the renowned Kobori Enshu and is one of the finest gardens of the period, with large ponds crossed by a covered walkway. In the northern pond is a 'turtle' island, while in the southern section is a rocky 'crane' island. A small, four-pillared structure, the 'Moon Viewing Pavilion' (*Kangetsu-dai*), was created for viewing the moon's reflection on the surface of the ponds. Within the garden are several tea houses, two of which are reached by steps mounting the hillside. The *Kasa-tei* (Umbrella House) and *Shigure-tei* (Rain Shower House) were designed by Sen-no-Rikyu, the famous sixteenth-century tea master. The *Kasa-tei* derivers its name from the ceiling made from bamboo and branches, which are woven in a pattern similar to a traditional Japanese umbrella. The two tea houses are connected by a wooden corridor.

Covered walkway across the pond.
Kodai-ji.

Bibliography

Allbright, Bryan, and Tindale, Constance, *A Path through the Japanese Garden* (Crowood, 2000)

Barrie, Anmarie, *The Professional's Book of Koi* (TFH Publication, 1992)

Borja, Erik, *Zen Garden* (Ward-Lock, 1999)

Brickell, Christopher (ed.), *The A to Z Encyclopedia of Garden Plants* (Dorling Kindersley, 2003)

Davidson, A.K., *Zen Gardening* (Hutchinson, 1982)

Dee, Jonathan, *Feng Shui for the Garden* (Caxton Publishing, 2000)

Engel, Heino, *Measure and Construction of the Japanese House* (Charles E. Tuttle, 1994)

Gustafson, Herb, *The Art of Japanese Gardens* (David & Charles, 1999)

Hale, Gill, *The Feng Shui Garden* (Aurum Press, 1998)

Harte, Sunniva, *Zen Gardening* (Pavilion Books, 1999)

Haslam, Gillian (ed.), *The Big Book of Outdoor DIY* (New Holland Publishing, 1997)

Horton, Alvin, *Creating Japanese Gardens* (Ortho Books, 1989)

Hoshikawa, Isao, *Elements of Japanese Gardens* (Graphic-sha Publishing, 1990)

Itoh, Teiji, *The Gardens of Japan* (Kodansha International, 1998)

Japanese Garden Research Association, *Create Your Own Japanese Garden* (Graphic-sha Publishing, 1995)

Jay, Roni, *Feng Shui in Your Garden* (HarperCollins, 1998)

Kawagushi, Yoko, *Serene Gardens* (New Holland Publishers, 2000)

Keane, Marc P., *Japanese Garden Design* (Charles E. Tuttle, 1996)

Lawrence, Mike (ed.), *Garden Brickwork* (New Holland Publishers, 1989)

Main, Alison, and Platten, Newell, *The Lure of the Japanese Garden* (Wakefield Press, 2002)

Nitschke, Günter, *Japanese Gardens* (Benedikt Taschen Verlag, 1993)

Ohashi, Haruso, *Japanese Garden* (Graphic-sha Publishing, 1986)

Prescott, David, *The Bonsai Handbook* (New Holland Publishers, 2001)

Recht, Christine, and Wetterwald, Max F., *Bamboos* (Timber Press, 1998)

Richards, Betty W., and Kaneko, Anne, *Japanese Plants: Know Them and Use Them* (Shufunotomo Co., 1995)

Rico Nos, Michiko, and Freeman, Michael, *The Modern Japanese Garden* (Octopus Publishing, 2003)

Seike, Kiyoshi and Kudō, Masanobu, *A Japanese Touch for Your Garden* (Kodansha International, 1992)

Skinner, Archie, and Arscott, David, *The Stream Garden* (Ward-Lock, 1996)

Slawson, David A., *Secret Teachings in the Art of Japanese Gardens* (Kodansha International, 1991)

Suzuki, Osamu, and Yoshikawa, Isai, *The Bamboo Fences of Japan* (Graphic-sha Publishing, 1998)

Takei, Jirō, and Keane, Marc P. (translators), *The Sakuteiki: Visions of the Japanese Garden*

Treib, Marc, and Herman, Ron, *A Guide to the Gardens of Kyoto* (Kodansha International, 2003)

Vertrees, J.D., *Japanese Maples* (Timber Press, 1998)

Waring, Philippa, *The Feng Shui of Gardening* (Souvenir Press, 1998)

Wilson, Andrew, *The Creative Water Gardener* (Ward-Lock, 1995)

Woolman, Jack, *A Plantman's Guide to Chrysanthemums* (Ward-Lock, 1989)

Yoshikawa, Isao, *Japanese Gardening in Small Spaces* (JOIE/Japan Publications, 1996)

Yoshikawa, Isao, *The World of Zen Gardens* (Graphic-sha Publishing, 1991)

Index